Practical Enochian Magick

for the New Hermetics Adept

Jason Augustus Newcomb

Practical Enochian Magick

for the New Hermetics Adept

Jason Augustus Newcomb

The New Hermetics Press

Sarasota, FL

First published in 2007 by
The New Hermetics Press
P. O. Box 18111
Sarasota, FL 34276
www.newhermetics.com

ISBN: 978-0-6151-7709-0

Cover Design and typesetting by Fr∴ N. I. L.

Acknowledgements

I wish to thank many people who have contributed to my practical understanding of working with this material. Amongst them are Scott Lesser, Julie Bissell, Lia Maria Salciccia, Leonya Haskin and other brave practitioners, all my students who provided inspiration and insight, especially Giles Vint for constant assistance with research in the U. K.

I wish to dedicate this book to my wife **Jennifer** and my daughter **Aurora** who patiently allowed me to miss some family time in order to complete it.

Other Books by Jason Augustus Newcomb:

Nonfiction:

21st Century Mage (Weiser Books, 2002)
The New Hermetics (Weiser Books, 2004)
Sexual Sorcery (Weiser Books, 2005)

The Book of Magick Power (NHP, 2007)
The Enochian Magick Toolbook (NHP, 2007)
The Complete New Hermetics Manual and Workbook (NHP, 2007)
The Advanced Adept Manual and Workbook (NHP, 2007)
New Hermetics Equinox Journal Vol. 1 (forthcoming)

Fiction:

The Brotherhood of Light and Darkness (NHP, 2007)

Contents

Introduction:
Why Enochian Magick?

Many students inquire with me regularly about advanced magick, interested particularly in evocation and invocation of higher beings. In terms of advanced New Hermetics practices, the "Enochian" system of magick is, in my opinion, one of the best and most useful branches that can be engaged by the adept. It is of course not for everyone. But for those adepts who are interested in ritual, angelic communication, evocation, astral exploration and practical ceremonial magick the Enochian system offers a world that is so rich and vivid that it would take several lifetimes to explore it fully.[1] You will find angels and devils, Gods and monsters of all shapes and varieties in this work.

The Enochian system offers enough possibility for practical exploration and discovery that it is really just about the only advanced "magick" that one need seriously worry about. While I have and will provide instructions in some other advanced ceremonial magick, the Enochian system seems one of the cleanest and best available. Of course most of the general principles outlined in this manual could also be applied to other forms of ritual invocation and evocation such as the five books of the Lemegeton (Goetia etc.), Qabalistic or Planetary Angelical workings and so on. But there are several unique features to Enochian magick that make it particularly useful for the New Hermeticist, although I hope this small essay will be useful for anyone inter-

---

[1] There are of course a number of advanced mystical and spiritual practices for the adept of the New Hermetics with which you may be familiar, and the Enochian system is not a replacement for these. It is simply an additional avenue for magical and astral exploration.

ested in the subject of Enochian Magick generally as well. What makes Enochian magick so interesting and efficacious is:

- The Enochian System was received entirely from transhuman intelligences (angels), and the invocations are in an unknown (but quite real) language. Both of these facets lend power to the system, making it one that really connects your consciousness to other worlds.

- The names of the beings and places invoked specifically within the system are almost entirely without any cultural baggage[1], making the system quite universal, since these beings are simply expressions of archetypal consciousness in virtually its most pure form.

- The four watchtowers fit perfectly within the New Hermetics inner temple, thus providing fertile ground for expanding the work already begun earlier. So much of the Enochian material is elemental[2] in focus that the New Hermeticist will be quite at home integrating this system with the inner temple once it is understood.

- Enochian magick is highly systematized, making it quite user friendly once its apparent complexity has been reduced to simple comprehension.

- The Enochian System has many inherent ambiguities, opening up the possibilities for a great deal of experimentation, exploration and innovation. There are many "holes" in the

---

[1] It should be noted that there is in fact a great deal of cultural baggage within John Dee's original work, because he was a very devout Christian. This should by no means discourage the non-Christian or overly encourage the Christian reader. Some of the material received by Dee and Kelly was in fact quite heretical and difficult to reconcile with any orthodox Christian point of view.

[2] It is very possible to argue on this point, but I will leave it to the intrepid astral explorer rather than the theorists to settle the matter. More on this later.

system that need to be filled in by the individual practitioner. This entire book should be considered highly experimental. These techniques must be tried for yourself, and your own conclusions and variations drawn from these experiments.

A number of you are probably thinking that the Enochian magical world seems like a strange fit in a system that has up until this point been so free of sectarianism, and Enochian magick is rather specific. But the simple fact is that this is one of the most powerful systems of magick that you will encounter. As you work with these tools you will discover things changing around you dramatically. This work is something like grabbing a hold of a live battery and running the charge directly through your soul. And if you are unbalanced you will find your imbalances quickly coming to a head. Your fears, doubts and personal problems will quickly grow into crippling monsters. On the other hand, if you approach this work from a balanced and enlightened space, you will swiftly find the gates of heaven opening up before you. And this more beautifully and palpably than you can probably imagine at this moment. It is only after the work that you have conducted in the previous levels of the New Hermetics that I feel comfortable promoting this magick at all. If you are unsure that you can handle a powerful upsurge in your magical potency, please continue with your previous work until you feel ready to move on to this area.

That is not to say that all of this will happen automatically. You can easily just "go through the motions" with this work, and find it no more or less effective than any other form of occultism. But if you use the magical techniques that you have already learned in the previous New Hermetics work such as charging spaces, invoking archetypes, expanding consciousness, rising on the planes and many other tools, you will find these technologies exploding your previous conceptions when you combine them with the Enochian Angels.

Enochian magick was actually one of the first forms of magick that I discovered as a very young teenager. I purchased

Gerald Schueler's *Enochian Magic* at the same time that I purchased *The Sacred Magic of Abramelin the Mage*. It would be many years before I would make any kind of practical exploration of the latter book, but the Enochian system, though very complex, was one of the first things I ever explored. Many of my earliest personal rituals were based on Enochian magick, at least in part. I cannot say, in retrospect, that Gerald Schueler's books are necessarily the best Enochian instructional texts. They offer a fairly diluted version of the system, but that was what was available to me at the time, and the strange language and alphabet of the Enochian system would become a lifelong interest from that time on. For that I will always be grateful. Later, it was within a practical Enochian Working Group that my first ideas about *The New Hermetics* came into existence. So, in all, I have been studying and practicing Enochian magick in one form or another for over twenty years, and it has always been a part of my New Hermetics work, though sometimes hidden in the background.

But this is very much an experimental manual. Nothing in this book is set in stone whatsoever. I strongly encourage your own creativity and variations as you work through this material. I have not taught or encouraged the use of Enochian magick amongst any of my personal New Hermetics students yet. A few have worked it on their own, but this is the first time that I am attempting to construct a practical text on this subject. The methods you will find herein are my own idiosyncratic tools. You may find some of them helpful, and others less so. But either way you are sure to be pleasantly surprised by the potency of this system.

What makes this system so powerful? Well, we can look at this both spiritually and practically. From a spiritual perspective, this system is so effective because it was delivered directly by a group of angels to Dr. John Dee through his skryer Edward Kelly. The Enochian system first came into being in the 1580's through the mysticical adventures of these two alchemical researchers. Dee was a noted mathematician, philosopher, avid book collector, and astrologer to Elizabeth I, as well as a student of renaissance Hermeticism. Kelly was a gifted seer and alchemical enthusiast who, while working with Dee, basically received the whole system directly through a long series of visions. Dee did not go into his experiments with Kelly specifically seeking this system. Their adventure together began with some operations in crystal gazing, with a mind toward understanding the secrets of the universe and god's creation, but the spirits came into the crystal with an agenda of their own, and slowly revealed a hitherto unknown hierarchy of beings as well as a vast amount of material in their own "angelic" language including the well known 49 Keys or "Enochian Calls." It should be noted that Dee never viewed any of this as "magick" in its lower sense, but rather "spiritual exercises" conducted to mystically connect with the divine.

But the beings called in modern Enochian magick are called in their own language, by their own secret names, as revealed by the angels themselves. This lends an incredible potency to this system from a spiritual standpoint, because the angels themselves have told us how to contact them, and their own special magical names.

From a practical perspective, the very strangeness of the names of the spirits and their language puts one into an "otherworldly sort of consciousness," that allows one's sense of the solidity of the universe to loosen. This is the same effect produced by the "barbarous names" of evocation found in some other Hermetic magick. The long strings of sonorous and odd words tend to alter one's state rather automatically. There is something nearing a sort of logic in the way that the watchtowers are set up. But at the same time, the whole enterprise is entirely illogical forcing one's brain to "suspend disbelief." Additionally, the strong reputation that Enochian magick enjoys as a "powerful" and "dangerous" system lends subconscious potency to your workings.

But I really must emphasize that you will contact genuine intelligence and new worlds in this magick, and your experiences will transform you. At first, these experiences may be fleeting, but you will soon find yourself changing in subtle and sometimes not so subtle ways. A quote from my journal perhaps says it best, "I must say I am feeling somewhat odd, as if this practice is leaving me somehow altered. I feel like perhaps there is no real coming back from this other dimension completely."

The system of angelic communication received by Dee and Kelly has obviously continued to be explored after their deaths by later generations of magical explorers. Some say the techniques were incorporated into the Rosicrucian movement of the 17th and 18th centuries, and there is certainly evidence that Dee traveled extensively in the areas where the Rosicrucian manifestos appeared a few years later. But this is for now mere educated guessing and speculation. However, it is a fact that due to a number of cypher manuscripts outlining rituals that contained both Rosicrucian and Enochian elements that this magical system receives so much attention today. These cipher documents inaugurated the birth of the organization known as the Order of the Golden Dawn. The Golden Dawn initiations all feature the four watchtower tablets, and the practical magick of the order largely centers around Enochian work. The Golden Dawn vastly elaborates the system delivered by the angels into a synthesis of Hermetic Magick as a whole including relationships to the Tarot, astrology, geomancy, qabalah and even the Egyptian Gods. The result is something that only vaguely resembles Dee's original material. However, the Golden Dawn techniques are still very useful. Even if they in some cases seem to garble the original Dee material, they offer a convenient way of approaching the system that does seem to work quite powerfully. Aleister Crowley is the only modern adept since the time of Dee and Kelly who has ever published "Enochian" visions that rival those of Kelly. His work was based almost entirely on the Golden Dawn techniques, so we can fairly safely suppose that the Golden Dawn elaborations do not automatically negate the effectiveness of the system in any way.

But much of the elaboration is extraneous and just makes a system that is already a bit daunting into something that is unnecessarily confusing. What you will find in these pages is a fusion of some of the Golden Dawn techniques with a lot of the original instructions of Dee's angels added back into the system and of course the expected simplification, reductionism and non-sectarian verbiage of the New Hermetics. I have tried to honor both approaches, the original as well as the Golden Dawn approach in this book. As much as possible I have woven the original work back into the Golden Dawn elaborations. I have also added many modern insights into the practice. The conscientious magick user will find a most potent approach to Enochian Magick presented simply and clearly in the following pages. Some of the raw information in this manual has been presented in other books, but I hope I have organized it in a way that will assist you in bringing this system to life in a simple and effective way.

There are three branches of practical Enochian magick as it has evolved into its modern forms.

- The Four Watchtowers- a series of lettered squares related to the four directions and/or the four elements that reveal the names of a multitude of archetypal beings (angels) of various kinds and ranks.

- The Thirty Aethyrs- a hierarchy of concentric spiritual planes or spheres surrounding the phenomenal universe that may be explored astrally resulting in various mystical and magical experiences, and a series of ninety-one governors of earthly regions.

- The 49 Heptarchical "Bonorum" Angels- a set of "planetary" angels with accompanying magical squares that can be invoked for diverse purposes. Talismans can also be constructed from the letter squares related to them.

Some would say that this last is really a separate magical system altogether, but since it has the same basic character as the other two branches, shares the same alphabet, and came from the same series of operations between Dee and Kelly it only seems fair to include it in the scheme. The heptarchic system is also directly connected to the rest through the Sigillum Dei Aemeth and the Holy Table, which are discussed at length in the appendices. Many modern writers, taking their cue from the Golden Dawn, have ignored the Heptarchic branch of Dee and Kelly's magick, and it is high time that some modern magicians really start to explore it practically and experimentally. I must admit that my own practical exploration with the Heptarchia has been much smaller than my other experiences, but I will provide you with the practical information that I possess.

I should also mention that the order in which Dee received these angelic systems was in reverse order to the manner in which it is being presented in this work. He received the Heptarchic system first, the keys, aethyrs and the governors second, and the four watchtowers third.

This book is by no means an exhaustive treatise on the work of Dee and Kelly. I will not extensively discuss the history of the system or the story of its two magi, I will not discuss the structure of the "angelic" language much, or any other background materials. This is a practical manual for practical occultists. It is designed to help you actually perform powerful invocations quickly and relatively easily. If you are interested in more academic information on the system I encourage you to examine the bibliography for many useful references. I suggest that you read through this book carefully before beginning your work. There is practical advice through all three sections that will help you to work with this system practically and effectively.

This magical system is a "technical" method of opening up communication with a vast array of visions and intelligences that share our world. What it offers above all is a map or meaningful plan of approach. Visions are not particularly hard to come by, but those that change your life are priceless.

Part One

The Magick of the four Watchtowers

Chapter One
The Temple and Implements

I have been accused in some quarters of reducing occultism to a series of daydreams, that I don't teach "real" magick because there are no physical ceremonies in *The New Hermetics*. This couldn't be further from reality. My whole purpose for writing has always been to encourage the actual practice of occultism. The New Hermetics is only one facet of anyone's magical palette. It is a set of tools for equilibrium and a set of magical and mystical tools that take into account many modern consciousness theories and practices. Anyone who has actually worked through the New Hermetics exercises knows their efficacy in making real transformations both inner and outer. What's more, many New Hermetics students do use physical ritual regularly, some performing traditional rites, others adapting the New Hermetics formulae into modern physical ritual actions.

And now that many New Hermetics students are getting into more specifically advanced work, some rudimentary physical ritual actions will become useful. As you begin your work with Enochian magick I highly suggest that you set up a physical temple with a physical altar and physical magical tools. To some this may seem strange, in the world of modern magick the "empty-handed gesture" is often viewed as the more advanced, and it might seem like a step backward to conduct physical rituals when you have become so adept at inner work and accomplishing magical tasks in a fully functional inner temple. However, now that you have so powerfully set up your inner workings, you will find that outer workings will be much more effective than if you had worked the other way around. You could simply proceed forward maintaining an entirely inward and meditative path, but with this work physical ritual will help in creating an environment conducive to success. And you can eventually conduct your work more or less completely in your inner temple. But as you get started, a physical temple will greatly assist you in focusing, anchoring and amplifying your work.

This temple does not have to be an entire room of your house solely and elaborately dedicated to magick, although this would be ideal. But just an uncluttered area will do fine. As long as you have room to walk around your altar, your circle can be whatever size your lifestyle can accommodate. The basic set up for your altar can be as simple as the four elemental weapons: wand, cup, dagger and disk. For those of you who have gone through the New Hermetics initiation you are familiar with another set of elemental representations: candle, cup, rose and disk. These could be substituted as well, at least until you can acquire suitable weapons.

Building a magical circle can be fairly painless. The following is sufficient.

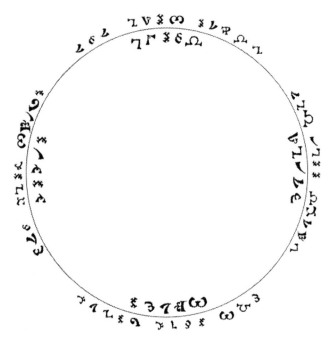

DIAGRAM 1- ENOCHIAN MAGICK CIRCLE

The names around the perimeter are from the "Tablet of Union" and the "Twelve Names of God" from the Four Watchtowers. You can draw them in chalk or tape them down, whatever is convenient for you. The construction of this sort of circle can be accomplished quite easily in less than an hour. You could simply create an unadorned circle if you wish as well, but adding "names of power" will lend an air of potency to your work. I don't recommend a merely "psychic" circle. Since you are conducting physical ritual, you may as well take this one small extra step. Laying a magical circle will ground this work, containing your focused energy and consecrating the physical location of your rituals. It should be noted that it is unclear whether, and probably unlikely that, Dee's work was conducted in a circle anything like this. There is a diagram depicting a circlular emblem with the twelve names holy mystical names of God on banners around the circle, but this is never explicitly discussed as a part of the magical process. Most conjuring from this time period was conducted in magical circles, but Dee always considered his work to be "spiritual exercises" rather than conjuring in any sense. This was of course at least partially connected with the ever-looming presence of the Holy Inquisition at that time. But it seems unlikely that he used a circle.

Your altar can be any convenient small square table, covered in a red cloth. This can also be the Holy Table discussed in part three and appendix D, or you could use your own altar if you have one from previous work. I do suggest that you construct the Holy Table if you are going to be regularly conducting Enochian work. This table design was delivered to Dee and Kelly through the angels, and was considered requisite for the work. For my first real Enochian experiments I followed Lon Duquette's "dare to be lazy" advice, and made a table by photocopying and blowing up an image of the holy table and pasting the sheets to a piece of foam board which I placed atop my own altar. I believe that we used this "table" in the Enochian work group I formed in the late nineties, and it may still be in the possession of Knights Templar Oasis, OTO in Salem, Mass-achusetts. Do you absolutely need to have this table in order to proceed? No. I have conducted fairly successful work without it. But conducting your work in a space that contains the proper symbolic elements will add tremendously to the effectiveness of your operations.

My most recent work has been conducted in a temple space in which I have not only the Holy Table, but the wax Sigillum Dei Aemeth[1] on the center of the table with a skrying stone on top, and four small wax Sigillae supporting the feet. Does this make my magick more effective? I'm not absolutely sure, but it certainly makes me *feel* like it is more effective. All of these items can be useful for focusing your attention on the nature of your work. There may also be some real magical benefit to these pieces of ritual furniture. They were very carefully and painstak-ingly communicated by the angels that delivered this system, and I have found that my experiences with Enochian magick have been much more dramatic and powerful when I have worked in a temple set up in a mostly traditional manner. This may of course just be because of its subconscious effect on my expectations, but this shouldn't be ignored. You are trying to open a gateway into another world. Anything you do to get the deeper parts of your consciousness involved will be useful. If you have a Sigillum Dei Aemeth (and/or a gazing crystal), these may be at the center of the altar, but these are not entirely necessary for most of the work as it is designed in this book. Still, if you have the skills to make one (or five), it is an empowering piece of ritual furniture.[2]

Diagrams of the four watchtowers can be situated on the walls or on your altar, though this is not a necessity. Dee almost assuredly did not have this sort of set up, as these watchtowers were lists of names for him, and did not have the talismanic qua-lity that we often assign to them today.

---

[1] See Appendix C.

[2] A set of wax seals, one large and four small ones can now be obtained from me online. Visit www.newhermetics.com for more information.

The four elemental weapons (wand, sword [or dagger], cup, and disk) can be arranged on your altar facing the appropriate elemental directions. Or you could use the weapons from the New Hermetics self-initiation if you are familiar with that ritual. They are in parentheses below.

Air- East- Dagger (or rose)
Fire- South- Wand (or candle)
Water- West- Cup
Earth- North- Disk

None of these tools are part of Dee's original system at all, but they form useful "anchors" to the states and energies of the elements with which you are connecting. You will use these weapons at various stages of ceremony to invoke and direct energy. A simple method for consecrating your ritual tools can be found in *The Book of Magick Power*.

Incense and colored candles appropriate to the energies you are invoking can also be used. Again, these are not at all called for by Dee's original work, but they can be powerful tools for transforming your consciousness and opening up to the subtle realms.

You should also note that there is a full-color companion volume to this present book containing colored illustrations of the four watchtowers, the tablet of union, the Heptarchia Mystica, and "scrolls" of the angelic keys as well as various other items pertinent to your practical ritual exploration of this system. This *Enochian Magick Toolbook* is a sort of "starter kit" that will make it possible for you to begin conducting your experiments quickly and easily. There are also further resources listed in Appendix E.

Chapter Two
The Magus and the Skryer

The most common way for Enochian Magick to be practiced is with two or more people, one reciting the conjurations (and often acting as a scribe to record the experience), with another acting as a skryer, sitting passively, entering into the visionary state while staring into a crystal or simply having a vision with eyes closed.

The tradition of seer or medium and guiding adept goes back to antiquity. We see it in the techniques of the spiritualists. We see it in the work of Aleister Crowley, the Hermetic Brotherhood of Luxor and Paschal Beverly Randolph. We see it in the work of Dee and Kelly and other Renaissance magi. We see it in medieval and even more ancient texts such as the Greek magical papyri that call for a child as seer. We even see it going all the way back the Oracle at Delphi, where the pythoness entered trance and the priests interpreted her vision.

This is a very effective method of working, but not everyone has a willing or able assistant capable of performing either role. As an experienced consciousness adept you should find it fairly easy to quickly enter into a visionary state after conducting ritual work on your own, so the additional magician is not really a necessity for the New Hermetics Adept. I will also later provide you with a very non-traditional but highly useful technique involving recording your experience electronically that may further assist you in solitary work.

In any case, your previous inner work should make skrying fairly automatic, you can simply go into your inner temple as you sit down after the invocations, and your visions can unfold from there. I have also recorded some CDs (and may someday release them) with the Enochian keys that I sometimes use after preliminary ritual. If you Know, Will, Dare and can keep Silent about it, you could easily use something like this in your work if you enjoy working that way. The fundamentally important part of the work is the visionary communication with the invoked beings, and we will discuss this and all other practicalities of ceremonial work throughout the rest of this book.

If you do have a willing and able partner, by all means enjoy that relationship and conduct your work with one acting as the ceremonialist, and the other entering the altered state and acting as seer. I still recommend that you consider recording your experiments, and that the seer may want to verbalize every stray experience that comes into the vision. Some of these images, feelings and thoughts may seem at the time irrelevant, but later turn out to be some of the most significant parts of the experience!

Chapter Three
Dee and his Angels

In his lifetime, John Dee was considered one of the greatest intellects of the age. He was a true polymath who was consulted for his knowledge, both sholarly and occult, on numerous issues by monarchs, nobles and adventurers all over Europe. His expertise in astronomy, navigation, mathematics, geography, theology, statecraft and even theatrical mechanics were legendary from the time he was a young man. But he was also viewed with mistrust and sometimes derision, why? The answer is because he talked to angels. In the sixteenth century, often little distinction was made between such activities and conjuring demons. By the time of his death his importance was already disappearing from the annals of conventional history. Why? The answer is because he talked to angels.

Despite Dee's profound influence on the english Renaissance, up until the twentieth century, there was not a single favorable biography of Dee by any conventional scholar. Why? The answer is because he talked to angels. There has been a great increase in scholarship on John Dee in the last forty years. His reputation is slowly being restored, but even amongst those scholars who support Dee's place in history, the angelic conferences are most often viewed as a strange episode that marred an otherwise bright life. Scholars such as Deborah Harkness try to take a neutral view, explaining that activities such as talking with angels, although perhaps absurd from a modern view, were a stage in the growth of scientific thought in the sixteenth century. Although the polarity of the dismissal has almost reversed,

Dee's angel work is still largely viewed with the same derision it has always received.

And yet here you are reading a book about a magical system based on his angelic conferences. It is only amongst we half-mad occultists that his magical work has been taken seriously, and it has always been taken very seriously. It has been preserved through the centuries, practiced in secret, and it's reputation as a "powerful" system has mushroomed into hero worship in the world of modern occultism.

But the intentions that most occultists have when they approach Enochian magick are very different from Dee's intentions. Dee sought to understand the mysteries of the manifest universe in a time when what we consider "science" did not yet exist. The Earth was still the center of a very small universe with seven heavenly spheres that led to God. The universe was almost universally thought to be only a few thousand years old. God certainly created the world in seven days. The return of Jesus was unquestionably immanent. It was under these conditions that Dee sought deeper insight into the "book of nature" through the only channel he thought available, the angels of this creation.

Modern occultists look at the world through far different eyes. Most view the universe in terms of modern scientific theories including usually at least a vague familiarity with quantum mechanics, relativity, and an understanding that space is most likely infinite. The place of angels is fairly unclear in this worldview. But Enochian magick still enjoys a powerful reputation. Modern occultists most usually approach Enochian magick for one of two reasons. Either they are interested in some sort of "proof" that there really are intelligent beings in spiritual planes, or they are interested in using these experiences (whether real or imaginary) to expand their "spiritual horizons" on a sometimes nebulous quest for "enlightenment," "magical power" or some other such thing. But the angels still answer our calls, even if our concepts of what exactly an angel is have dramatically changed or even disappeared into a murky meta-physical mental haze.

All three sections of the Enochian system introduce you to a vast array of otherworldly beings with a highly developed hier-archy and purpose for existence. The names of most of these beings are not to be found anywhere else in history. They are totally unique to this system of magick. Many of the names of these beings are not even pronounceable in any normal sense, being just strings of consonants such as CZNS, the first servient or lesser angel in the air of air subquadrant of the eastern watchtower of air. The reason for this strangeness is most likely because this angelic language is not a spoken language at all. Angels do not have vocal chords after all. Dee himself notes to the angels, "I do think you have no organs or Instruments apt for voice, but are meere spirituall and nothing corporall, but have the power and property from God to insinuate your message or meaning to ear or eye [and] man's imagination shall be that they hear and see you sensibly." The "Enochian" language is a series of talismanic hieroglyphs that open up the lines of communi-cation with these beings.

And it is quite possible and not even particularly difficult to make contact. These beings are very capable of assisting you in the transformation of life and consciousness. But you may be wondering in the back of your mind whether there is really actually anything useful to be gained from invoking angels. Why bother? You may be slightly put off by the concept of working with angelic beings altogether because you try to view the world from a non-dual perspective. If we are all one then what is the point of invoking angels at all? I tend to share that basic view, at least on alternate Tuesdays, but it must be remembered that we may all be one, but we also have a conventional existence that is not negated by the realization of our essential oneness. Angels, while similarly part of the one, also have conventional existence. And what is interesting about the perspective of these angels is that while they possess knowledge that is far beyond our own conventional existence, it is confined to the unique area of the universe of which they are a part. The angels of the aerial places understand the elements of aerial life, but have little knowlege of the deep darkness beneath the earth and vice versa. In these places we can understand the transpersonal components of our being in their own contexts.

In order to speak to angels, it is necessary to be in a state of consciousness in which this sort of communication is a real possibility. For some this state is fairly easy to get into, for others it takes a bit more work. Reciting the Enochian keys in and of itself tends to help create this state. But the fundamentally important factor is to be in an exalted state, one in which your consciousness is "angelic." The initial New Hermetics course of practice (levels one through five) is designed to lead your consciousness to this kind of state naturally, through the gradual process of equilibrium and exaltation through numerous practical techniques. The tools for communion with cosmic consciousness in particular are extremely useful as preliminaries for Enochian magick. Now that you have conducted this work, getting into the angelic state should be a fairly simple matter. If you have not conducted this work, and do not wish to do so before conducting your Enochian magick, you can still invoke some sense of this state of cosmic consciousness as a preliminary.

Another critical factor is belief. If you do not believe that these angels exist as entities outside of your own consciousness then you will most likely only communicate with your own subconscious in these practices. While there is little harm in such an activity, it seems a bit pointless to go through elaborate ceremonies to do so. If you believe that it is possible and probable that you can establish communication with real intelligence beyond your personal consciousness then a universe of infinite potential is open to you.

Contacting these beings will help you to understand yourself and your universe more than you can imagine. But really the reason for contacting these angels is for the most part quite similar to the reason why a person composes a poem, looks at the stars through a telescope or decides to dance. The desire for the experience is the motivation, plain and simple. There may be an urge for knowledge, expression, or power, but at its core it is just a desire to experience that which you will to experience. No other explanation is really necessary. The "art" involved here is one with a largely spiritual aim. These beings contain in themselves a theurgic component and a revelatory component. You will quite likely receive information that relates to vast nonpersonal themes. This may be the unconscious reason you are drawn to this magick. The angels may be calling for you. In this you must be cautious because it is very easy for unbalanced forces (either within or without) to disguise themselves as messengers of the light.

I have found that the Angels of this system are very responsive to the call of the adept. These angels are actively working for the evolution of humanity, and are very willing to help you in any matter that will further that cause. Do not be surprised if you find yourself offered a higher calling as a result of this work.

There are also a number of useful ways of approaching these beings for specific purposes. This is a system of practical magick after all. I think the best way to look at this is to see these angelic contacts as being for the purpose of seeking to accomplish your will more effectively, or more appropriately the universal will, and your unique place within the unfolding of the universe. You can seek the answers to these big questions from these angels, and gain invaluable insight from the answers. The answers you receive will of course be idiosyncratic to you alone, and will of course be colored by the particular area of their expertise and will need to be augmented by advice from angels of other areas and your own common sense by all means.

These angels are also personifications of the rudimentary building blocks of the phenomenal universe, and are capable of accomplishing quite practical things in your life as well. Of course this is subject to the limits of their sphere of influence and your own limitations. This kind of practical Enochian magick should be used with caution. Calling upon the primal spiritual forces of the universe to accomplish one's passing whims is something so foolish that hopefully this warning is superfluous for the adept. It is something like writing to your senator because you want a better parking place at work. Use the simple tools of the practitioner and philosopher level of the New Hermetics for such things. Reserve this work for issues that relate to large-scale issues of importance to your life's work and vital necessity. Of course this is a highly subjective matter and your own wisdom will have to be your guide. It may be that a new parking space is fundamentally important to the whole future existence of the universe.

In such cases, the success or failure of the operation will be a good guide. If you ask an angel to help you win a court case, and you do not win, then perhaps that "negative" conclusion is the one that will ultimately serve the universal economy more effectively. In these matters you must take into account a huge number of variables. What is best for "you" is not necessarily best for the universe. And in the scale of things you will not find such acts effective.

And a few such ineffective operations may render your faith in this magick shaken to the point that it may become operatively inert. Doubt may start to plague each conjuration, and your contact with the angels could eventually be severed altogether. So, be intelligent in your choices. These warnings apply more to working with these beings in a practical way. The quest for knowledge, although possessing dangers of its own, does not have quite as much danger of magical backfire. The dangers in the quest for knowledge include delusions of grandeur, the messiah complex, and 331 other obsessions along the way. Do not be surprised if you begin to discover universal themes in your visions that do not directly relate to you and your personal problems. These beings are not personal playthings but a fountain of higher consciousness that has its own agenda.

However, in these matters you will still want to take on an attitude of authority. You are an autonomous being who is able to direct these angels through the force of the hierarchy of which they are a part. As an adept, you have made contact with cosmic consciousness, a connection to the ultimate oneness of things, and it is with this authority that you are attempting to contact these hierarchies of intelligence. You will know the names of the beings that are hierarchically above the beings you contact, and you will instruct these beings to do your will by invoking the names of their superiors. It is very much like a military operation. Because you are in touch with the absolute authority (cosmic consciousness) you can speak in the name of the generals (divine names) which are in authority over the majors, captains, lieutenants etc. (the angels) and tell them what you wish to have accomplished as a representative of the absolute authority. But this must be done gently. Arrogance on any plane will cause the angels to revolt, and your magical progress to cease. By now you have hopefully made enough progress toward an enlightened state that you are not going to attempt to use this authority for capricious ends of any kind. This will deteriorate your adepthood and your connection with these angels. These matters will all become clearer as you progress.

But I'm sure the question still remains in some of your minds, "But are these angels real separate beings, or are they *really* just a part of my unconscious mind?" The principles and axioms of magick have changed slowly (and sometimes quickly) over time and the meaning and purpose of magick has changed along the way. The ancient Persian Magi viewed the unseen world in vastly different terms than the Medieval sorcerer, and the Medieval sorcerer saw the spirit world in a different light than the Renaissance conjurers. Likewise, the Victorian era revival of magick viewed the subject in new ways, unfamiliar to any of their predecessors, and our current operating principles are continuing to evolve around us as modern adepts. I will suggest that you set the question aside entirely for the moment and after twenty or so advanced experiments you can decide if the question is *really* even relevant to you anymore.

Chapter Four
The Four Watchtowers

The first part of the system of John Dee's angelic magick that we will explore is the angels related to the four watchtowers of the four directions, east, west, north and south. These are most usually considered to be the angels of the four elements by modern magicians.

DIAGRAM 2- THE FOUR WATCHTOWERS AND BLACK CROSS

Diagram 2 is the "Great Table." It depicts the four watchtowers of the universe connected by the "black cross" or "tablet of union." Each quadrant of the diagram is one of the watchtowers. Each of the letters in the four watchtowers was received one at a time by Dee through the skrying of Kelly. The left uppermost quadrant is the watchtower of the east (air), the upper right is the watchtower west (water), the lower left is the watchtower of the north (earth) and that on the lower right is the watchtower of the south (fire). And each of these watchtowers is subdivided again into air of air, water of air earth of air etc. as depicted in diagram 3.

AIR   WATER

Air of Air	Water of Air	Air of Water	Water of Water
Earth of Air	**Fire of Air**	**Earth of Water**	**Fire of Water**
Air of Earth	**Water of Earth**	**Air of Fire**	**Water of Fire**
Earth of Earth	**Fire of Earth**	**Earth of Fire**	**Fire of Fire**

EARTH   FIRE

DIAGRAM 3- THE ELEMENTS IN THE WATCHTOWERS

It should be noted that all of these elemental and subelement-al categorizations are accretions from the Golden Dawn. Dee and his communicating spirits refer to the watchtowers repeatedly as merely relating to the four directions, North, South, East and West. While these directions are often associated with the ele-ments in question in both modern and ancient literature, Dee did not seem to think of them in this way at all. Or if he did, he does-n't seem to mention it in his journals. The interesting thing about these differences between the Dee originals and the Golden Dawn interpretations is that they seem to pose no problem in the practical use of the system. For those who think of the work as elemental, it is elemental. For those who think otherwise, it oper-ates otherwise. The matter has been further confused by several modern authors offering different elemental attributions such as using the zodiacal attributions: East-Fire, South-Earth, West-Air, North-Air, or even perhaps Crowley's attributions from Liber V vel Reguli. All of this is worthy of exploration, but certainly does not offer "Truth" with a capital "T." There is no correct answer, except the one that yields useful and meaningful application in your life, when actually using this system.

For many reasons, I feel it is most convenient to view the four watchtowers in the basic way that the Golden Dawn oriented the system. It offers ease of use in numerous ways that may become clear as we proceed. It connects you to the egregore established by the Golden Dawn. It also fits very conveniently into the inner temple work of the New Hermetics. And in the words of Aleister Crowley, "Convenience is our canon of truth."[1] One aspect that makes the elemental conventions particularly useful for our practical work is that it provides some differences in character and function within the watchtowers. Without this, there is little reason to work with one watchtower over another unless your magick is somehow specifically related to the compass points.

---

[1] Crowley, Aleister. *Magick: Liber ABA* p. 499-500

(For instance if you wish to bewitch your neighbor's cows on the eastern border of your property...)

In some places I will distinguish between Golden Dawn variations and the Dee originals. In other places I will not. The system "works" either way, and we will retain the modern conventions that are useful.

Nonetheless, I suggest that you see these "elemental" aspects of the system as convenient guideposts rather than as the core of what these watchtowers represent. Saying that the "Watchtower of the East" is connected to the element of "Air" can be most usefully viewed as a method of categorization. It is a part of human nature and hermetic practice to categorize things in this way. Any time we meet a system of four, it is only natural to find correspondences with other quadratic symbol structures such as the four elements. Likewise, when we meet systems involving seven factors, we look for ways in which these correspond with the seven planets, or the musical notes, or the days of the week etc. But to think these are "the same thing" is probably going a bit far. Since you are already familiar with the elemental directions within your inner temple, I suggest you use these attributions in your Enochian work. But the choice is ultimately up to you. The work in this portion of the book is largely elemental in basis, but I don't want you to ignore the fact that this system was originally directional, rather than elemental.

Most importantly I would suggest that you allow yourself to experience these visions as free from expectation as possible. Allow the angels to teach you their purposes and natures. The suggestions in this book should not be forced upon these angels but rather used as guidelines. These angels will be very malleable to your expectations and direction. Try to be open to truth rather than preconceived notions. In the words of the late great Enochian mage Benjamin Rowe, "They strive always to conform their actions to the will of the magician. This means that if the magician enters into their realm with specific expectations, they will seek to fulfill those expectations, even if it means overlaying a true picture of the realm with a false one." This might not be disastrous in every circumstance, but it is certainly not a habit you ought to nurture.

Those of you familiar with modern witchcraft have probably heard the term "watchtower" several times before, used in older books to describe the elements and the four directions. You may have even wondered what the term "watchtower" referred to. Well, in fact it refers to this system of Enochian magick. Gerald Gardner drew the name directly from the Golden Dawn description of these very watchtowers when constructing his early witchcraft rites. Many more recent witchcraft books have discarded the term, but most written before the nineties use it in temple openings. It makes one wonder if it was discarded when wiccans realized that this linked witchcraft a bit too closely with "ceremonial magick." But for our purposes these four watchtowers or elemental tablets (I will use these names interchangeably) are in essence ciphers containing a hierarchy of names. Each of the watchtowers yields the names of a multitude of intelligent trans-human entities by manipulating and reading the letters in different ways. In the pages that follow I will provide detailed lists and tables of these beings. Although you can view the watchtower tablets as a sort of odd, two dimensional holograph, or as maps of the elemental worlds, the most important thing to understand about these tablets is that they are first and foremost lists of names.

These beings have their existence in the astral plane (and perhaps higher) in the four directions. Your inner temple pro-vides the perfect place for you to contact these beings directly and easily. Essentially the four walls of your inner temple open up into these elemental regions, and through the use of the formulas of Enochian magick you will be able to invoke these beings into communication directly. These beings offer a perfect avenue for moving your magick into the transpersonal realm.

Each of the watchtowers contains a hierarchy consisting of:

• Three Great Mystical names of God ruling each watchtower

- A Great Angelic King
- Six Seniors or Elders
- Four Kerubic Archangels
- Sixteen Kerubic Angels
- Sixteen (or 64) Servient Angels
- Sixteen (or 64) Servient "Super" Angels
- Sixteen (or 32 or 128 or more) Kakodaimons

The numbers in parentheses represent some ambiguities in the system that will be discussed momentarily.

A Note on Lettering

If you have ever studied Enochian magick before you have probably noticed that in many books there are squares in the watchtowers that have more than one letter in them. This is because as Dee was working with his angelic communicators there were corrections made to the tablets over time, including changing the positions of the tablets themselves, and latter day "Golden Dawn" writers decided at some point to simply include all the possible variations of letters into their books. This is an unnecessary confusion. It seems most likely that the early Golden Dawn papers contained tablets with single letters, and that the multiple letters were added later by eager but misguided editors. Aleister Crowley's tablets as printed in the Equinox only contain one letter in each square, and his sources for his Enochian magick essays were Golden Dawn papers.

Many other writers on the subject seem to have chosen different lettering schemes for different sets of names and have proliferated multiple generations of errors. Throughout this book I will use the Raphael corrections of April 20, 1587. This means that there is only one letter in each square of the watchtowers, and all of the names of the various beings will be extractable from the tablets themselves in this book. Some authors have hesitated to adopt this final form, but there is really no reason to doubt this angelic communication while believing the others.

This will change a few names that you may be familiar with if you've studied this system before, and this may lend some slight confusion if you have other Enochian reference materials, but this is the most accurate way of representing the system in the final form presented by its creators/recipients. This will hopefully make the system more powerful and understandable.

The Tablet of Union

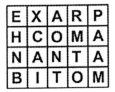

DIAGRAM 4- THE TABLET OF UNION

This "tablet" was received in a different manner than the other four. The angel Ave told Dee to isolate three names associated with the Tenth Aethyr (we'll talk more about the aethyrs later)

Lexarph
Comanan
Tabitom

He was told to remove the initial letter "L" and to list the remaining letters in sets of five. This was the result.

e x a r p
h C o m a
n a n T a
b i t o m

These letters were then put into the black cross as you can see if you refer to Diagram 2.

This is another area in which the Golden Dawn deviated significantly from the original Dee materials. The Golden Dawn associated this "Tablet of Union" as a whole with the fifth element of Spirit, and each line, which they considered the names of angels, associated with one of the four elements and one of the tablets.

exarp	air	east
hComa	water	west
nanTa	earth	north
bitom	fire	south

This causes a few significant effects on the system later. Of course, none of this seems present in Dee's diaries. But again, as I hope you will see soon, this convention is extremely useful and I will continue to use it.

But before you start getting confused and discouraged, let's move on to discuss the major forces within the four watchtowers. In the next chapter you will encounter numerous words that do not contain enough vowels to pronounce in any sensible way. There are multiple ways of approaching this. The Golden Dawn adepts added vowels based on Hebrew transliteration. This does not seem to be present in Dee's journals, which offer many pronunciation hints. It seems the general rule was to add an aspirated vowel sound to fill in the gap, most often it seems to be an "eh" or uh" sound. With a bit of practical exploration you will no doubt come to a workable manner of uttering the syllables. The phonetic guide to the keys in Appendix A should give you some sense of this process.

Chapter Five
Extracting the Angel Names from The Watchtowers

In this chapter I will quickly go through the names of the angels of the watchtowers. This aspect of the Enochian system has been written about so frequently that it is almost tempting to omit these rather dry lists of names. Nonetheless, for the sake of completeness, and because there are quite a few variations in the extant literature, I will briefly go over each of the sets of angel's names that are derived from the watchtowers.

Remember that these names are based on the corrected tablets, so they are slightly different than some of those published elsewhere. I have also chosen to adopt a few somewhat quirky Golden Dawn innovations that are variants from Dee's work. My reasons for this should be clear from the text.

In the next chapter we will take a closer look at their functions and personalities from a New Hermetics perspective, but for now here is a brief introduction to the hierarchy and the process of finding the names in each watchtower.

The Mystical Names of God

The first names to be extracted from the watchtowers are the twelve secret mystical names of God. This religious term should not alarm you, even if you are not a monotheist. Simply look at these names as keys that unlock the energies of the watchtowers. They are the names through which the angels of the tablets are commanded. This need not suggest any particular metaphysical or theological framework or theory.

Each watchtower contains three of these names- a name of three letters, a name of four letters, and a name of five letters. These names run horizontally in the central cross within each tablet.

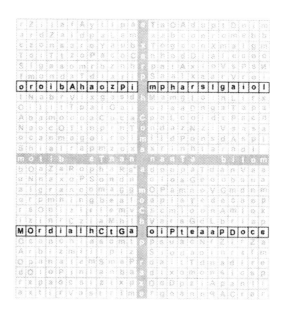

DIAGRAM 5 - 12 MYSTICAL NAMES

They are:

ORO IBAH AOZPI	EAST
MPH ARSL GAIOL	WEST
MOR DIAL HCTGA	NORTH
OIP TEAA PDOCE	SOUTH

These names open up the watchtowers and awaken the forces within them. They are the supreme names of power within each of the watchtowers, and you will use these names to begin each working with a watchtower, and you can also use these names to test any and all of the spirits. Some magicians have also reported success in conjuring and communicating with beings identified with these names. I have not experimented with this matter, so you will have to experiment for yourself if you are interested. However, there are so many other beings to communicate with that you can put this experiment off for quite a while!

The Great Kings

These are the ruling powers within each of the watchtowers, under the banners of the above Mystical Names of God. The Golden Dawn associated these beings with the planetary energy of the Sun within each of the tablets. This is not present in Dee, in which these names merely seem to be considered further mystical names of God used only in invocations of other beings. But many modern magicians have conjured these beings, and you may find yourself doing so as well. The names each contain eight letters, and are extracted in a spiral toward the center of the crosses like this:

DIAGRAM 6- THE FOUR KINGS

They are:

BATAIVAH	East
RAAGIOSL	West
ICZHIHAL	North
EDLPRNAA	South

The Twenty four Seniors

The names of twenty-four seniors or elders are also found within the central crosses, six in each watchtower. According to Dee's diaries, these seniors are the same twenty-four elders mentioned repeatedly in the Apocalypse of John.[1] The names of the seniors are drawn from each of the watchtowers out of the central cross, blossoming forth from the center of the crosses like this:

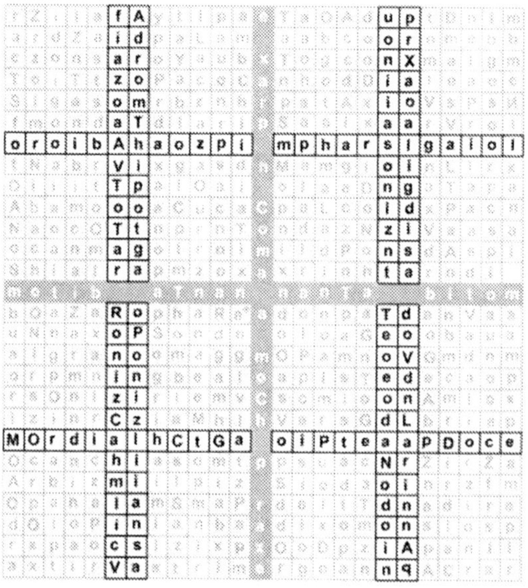

DIAGRAM 7- THE TWENTY-FOUR SENIORS

---

[1] Revelation 4:4, 4:10 , 5:5, 5:6, 5:8, 5:11, 5:14, 7:11, 7:13, 11:16, 14:3, 19:4.

These elders are said in Dee's notebooks to have all the wisdom of Solomon and more, and to deliver knowledge and judgment in human affairs (and perhaps in affairs beyond as well).

The Golden Dawn on the other hand assigned each of the seniors to energies of one of the six planets (other than the sun, which they associated with the King, as previously mentioned). This association brings some planetary force into the watchtowers, as well as a convenient way of distinguishing the seniors from each other. Without this classification, they are rather monolithically homogeneous sets of letters that resemble gibberish. Again, I suggest that you view these attributions more as guideposts than seeing them as parts of their essential nature.

These are their names, and the planets associated by the Golden Dawn:

East (Air)
HIPOTGA   - Saturn
AAOZAIF   - Jupiter
HABIORO   - Mars
AHAOZPI   - Venus
AVTOTAR   - Mercury
HTMORDA - Moon

West (Water)
LIGDISA   - Saturn
SAIINOV   - Jupiter
LSRAHPM   - Mars
SLGAIOL   - Venus
SONIZNT   - Mercury
LAOAXRP   - Moon

North (Earth)
LIIANSA   - Saturn
ACZINOR   - Jupiter
LAIDROM   - Mars
ALHCTGA   - Venus

AHMLICV   - Mercury
LZINOPO   - Moon

South (Fire)
ARINNAP   - Saturn
ADOEOET   - Jupiter
AAETPIO   - Mars
AAPDOCE   - Venus
ANODOIN   - Mercury
ALNDVOD   - Moon

For some reason, these are the beings most often called upon in modern Enochian magick and most people seem content with the planetary associations assigned to them by the Golden Dawn. In my opinion, the fact of their popularity is largely because of these specific associations with the planets, giving them an accessible "personality" and function. For example, if you are looking to increase your force and decisiveness in financial affairs, you might contact LAIDROM, the senior associated with Mars in the Earth tablet. This is just one simple example of the practical utility and convenience of the Golden Dawn attributions. Your own experiments in these matters will most effectively inform you of how best to approach these beings, but these planetary attributions can form a place to begin. There is a definite transpersonal quality to communications from these seniors, and the "filter" of the planetary correspondences may prove useful in categorizing your experiments. If you are conversing with one of these beings and you discover some other set of attributions, feel free to adopt it. Allow yourself to be open to new information of any kind. Again, it is easy to allow your expectations to cloud communication, or even to make genuine communication negligible. Make sure that you are not forcing your experiences to coincide with your expectations. This will severely limit your magical awakening.

Calvary Cross Names

Crosses are formed within each subquadrant of the tablets. Each of these crosses yields two names of power within the system. These names of power are used in conjurations of the Servient Angels, who we will discuss momentarily. The Servient Angel names are found in the squares beneath the horizontal arms of these crosses.

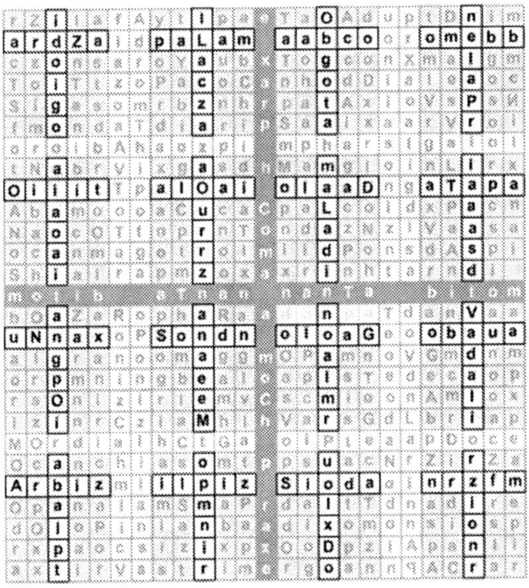

DIAGRAM 8- THE CALVARY CROSSES

The name of power that runs downward conjures these Servient Angels, and the name that reads across the horizontal arm of the cross forces the obedience of these angels. These are the names:

East (Air)

IDOIGO and ARDZA	Air subangle
LLACZA and PALAM	Water subangle
AIAOAI and OIIIT	Earth subangle
AOVRRZ and ALOAI	Fire subangle

49

West (Water)

OBGOTA and AABCO   Air subangle
NELAPR and OMEBB   Water subangle
MALADI and OLAAD   Earth subangle
IAAASD and ATAPA   Fire subangle

North (Earth)

ANGPOI and VNNAX   Air subangle
ANAEEM and SONDN   Water subangle
ABALPT and ARBIZ   Earth subangle
OPMNIR and ILPIZ   Fire subangle

South (Fire)

NOALMR and OLOAG   Air subangle
VADALI and OBAUA   Water subangle
UOLXDO and SIODA   Earth subangle
RZIONR and NRZFM   Fire subangle

Some magicians also regard these names as beings or angels in their own right and conjure them to communication as well. You can attempt communication with them if you wish, but they are most often simply used within conjurations of the Servient Angels.

Kerubic Angels and Archangels

The names of sixteen kerubic angels in each watchtower are formed from the four letters above the crosses in each of the subquadrants.

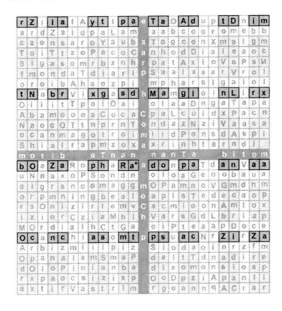

DIAGRAM 9- THE KERUBIC ANGELS

Four names are formed from each set of four letters by placing the first letter at the end of the new name to create four permutations, like this:

East (Air)

RZLA, ZLAR, LARZ, ARZL	Air subangle
YTPA, TPAY, PAYT, AYTP	Water subangle
TNBR NBRT, BRTN, RTNB	Earth subangle
XGSD, GSDX, SDXG, DXGS	Fire subangle

West (Water)

TAAD, AADT, ADTA, DTAA	Air subangle
TDIM, DIMT, IMTD, MTDI	Water subangle
MAGL AGLM, GLMA, LMAG	Earth subangle
NLRX, LRXN, RXNL, XNLR	Fire subangle

North (Earth)

BOZA, OZAB, ZABO, ABOZ	Air subangle
PHRA, HRAP, RAPH, APHR	Water subangle

51

OCNC CNCO, NCOC, COCN   Earth subangle
ASMT, SMTA, MTAS, TASM   Fire subangle

South (Fire)
DOPA, OPAD, PADO, ADOP   Air subangle
ANAA, NAAA, AAAN, AANA   Water subangle
PSAC SACP, ACPS, CPSA   Earth subangle
ZIZA, IZAZ, ZAZI, AZIZ   Fire subangle

Looking at these incomprehensible sets of syllables, hopefully you will begin to see why it is useful to split these beings up into elemental and subelemental categories. Without these filing systems, it would be rather hard to comprehend any difference between these beings.

However, these sets of angels are each ruled by an archangel whose name is found by appending a letter from the tablet of union to the first name from the set of four. For example, the archangel who rules RZLA, ZLAR, LARZ, ARZL is ERZLA. The letter "e" is drawn from "exarp" in the tablet of union.

Now, this is one of the most significant of those many areas in which there is a great deal of difference amongst various modern magicians. Dee's instructions from the angels are rather ambiguous, and there are at least two different reasonable ways of interpreting the directions, which give two different sets of angelic names. We will use the method adopted within the Golden Dawn, as it works best with the elemental interpretation of the watchtowers. This diverges significantly from Dee, and I will discuss this as well as other possibilities in Appendix B.

So, in drawing out these names, you will use the first letter of each of the lines of the tablet of union, according to the elements.

Exarp   Air
Hcoma   Water
Nanta   Earth
Bitom   Fire

So the names of the archangels, kerubic angels and their sub-quadrants are as follows:

East (Air):
ERZLA rules RZLA, ZLAR, LARZ, ARZL   Air subangle
EYTPA rules YTPA, TPAY, PAYT, AYTP   Water subangle
ETNBR rules TNBR, NBRT, BRTN, RTNB   Earth subangle
EXGSD rules XGSD, GSDX, SDXG, DXGS   Fire subangle

West (Water):
HTAAD rules TAAD, AADT, ADTA, DTAA   Air subangle
HTDIM rules TDIM, DIMT, IMTD, MTDI   Water subangle
HMAGL rules MAGL, AGLM, GLMA, LMAG   Earth subangle
HNLRX rules NLRX, LRXN, RXNL, XNLR   Fire subangle

North (Earth)
NBOZA rules BOZA, OZAB, ZABO, ABOZ   Air subangle
NPHRA rules PHRA, HRAP, RAPH, APHR   Water subangle
NOCNC rules OCNC, CNCO, NCOC, COCN   Earth subangle
NASMT rules ASMT, SMTA, MTAS, TASM   Fire subangle

South (Fire)
BDOPA rules DOPA, OPAD, PADO, ADOP   Air subangle
BANAA rules ANAA, NAAA, AAAN, AANA   Water subangle
BPSAC rules PSAC, SACP, ACPS, CPSA   Earth subangle
BZIZA rules ZIZA, IZAZ, ZAZI, AZIZ   Fire subangle

You can call these kerubic archangels in their own right, or more likely you can invoke their names to conjure the kerubic angels. This will be marked clearly in the practical section.

The Servient Angels

Below the arms of each of the calvary crosses are sixteen squares of letters. These letters each form the names of more angels, often called the Servient Angels.

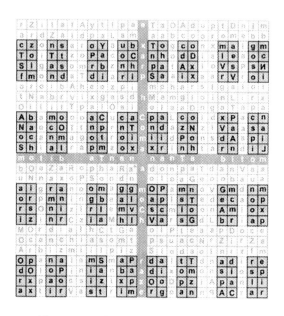

DIAGRAM 10- THE SERVIENT ANGELS

Dee recorded that there were four angels in each subquadrant, one four-lettered name for each line, read horizontally. This is yet another area of disagreement between the Dee diaries and the Golden Dawn. Within the Golden Dawn System, the number of angels in each subquadrant is sixteen, by permuting the letters of each name in the same way as the Kerubic angels. In my experience, I have found the permuted angels just as easy to contact. But this is certainly subject to more practical experimentation. So, of the following names, the first names are definitely certain, and the others a bit more uncertain:

East (Air)

CZNS...	ZNSC, NSCZ, SCZN	Air subangle
TOTT...	OTTT, TTTO, TTOT	Air subangle
SIAS...	IASS, ASSI, SSIA	Air subangle
FMND...	MNDF, NDFM, DFMN	Air subangle
OYVB...	YVBO, VBOY, BOYV	Water subangle
PAOC...	AOCP, OCP, CPAO	Water subangle

RBNH...	BNHR, NHRB, HRBN	Water subangle
DIRI...	IRID, RIDI, IDIR	Water subangle
ABMO...	BMOA, MOAB, OABM	Earth subangle
NACO...	ACON, CONA, ONAC	Earth subangle
OCNM...	CNMO, NMOC, MOCN	Earth subangle
SHAL...	HALS, ALSH, LSHA	Earth subangle
ACCA...	CCAA, CAAC, AACC	Fire subangle
NPNT...	PNTN, NTNP, TNPN	Fire subangle
OTOI ...	TOIO, OIOT, IOTO	Fire subangle
PMOX...	MOXP, OXPM, XPMO	Fire subangle

West (Water)

TOCO...	OCOT, COTO, OTOC	Air subangle
NHDD...	HDDN, DDNH, DNHD	Air subangle
PAAX...	AAXP, AXPA, XPAA	Air subangle
SAIX...	AIXS, IXSA, XSAI	Air subangle
MAGM...	AGMM, GMMA, MMAG	Water subangle
LEOC...	EOCL, OCLE, CLEO	Water subangle
VSSN...	SSNV, SNVS, NVSS	Water subangle
RVOI...	VOIR, OIRV, IRVO	Water subangle
PACO...	ACOP, COPA, OPAC	Earth subangle
NDZN...	DZNN, ZNND, NNDZ	Earth subangle
IIPO...	IPOI, POII, OIIP	Earth subangle
XRNH...	RNHX, NHXR, HXRN	Earth subangle
XPCN...	PCNX, CNXP, NXPC	Fire subangle
VASA...	ASAV, SAVA, AVAS	Fire subangle
DAPI...	APID, PIDA, IDAP	Fire subangle
RNIL...	NILR, ILRN, LRNI	Fire subangle

North (Earth)

AIRA...	IRAA, RAAI, AAIR	Air subangle
ORMN...	RMNO, MNOR, NORM	Air subangle
RSNI...	SNIR, NIRS, IRSN	Air subangle
IZNR...	ZNRI, NRIZ, RIZN	Air subangle
OMGG...	MGGO, GGOM, GOMG	Water subangle
GBAL...	BALG, ALGB, LGBA	Water subangle

RLMV...	LMVR, MVRL, VRLM	Water subangle
IAHL...	AHLI, HLIA, LIAH	Water subangle
OPNA...	PNAO, NAOP, AOPN	Earth subangle
DOOP...	OOPD, OPDO, PDOO	Earth subangle
RXAO...	XAOR, AORX, ORXA	Earth subangle
AXIR...	XIRA, IRAX, RAXI	Earth subangle
MSAP...	SAPM, APMS, PMSA	Fire subangle
IABA...	ABAI, BAIA, AIAB	Fire subangle
IZXP...	ZXPI, XPIZ, PIZX	Fire subangle
STIM...	TIMS, IMST, MSTI	Fire subangle

South (Fire)

OPMN...	PMNO, MNOP, NOPM	Air subangle
APST...	PSTA, STAP, TAPS	Air subangle
SCIO...	CIOS, IOSC, OSCI	Air subangle
VASG...	ASGV, SGVA, GVAS	Air subangle
GMNM...	MNMG, NMGM, MGMN	Water subangle
ECOP...	COPE, OPEC, PECO	Water subangle
AMOX...	MOXA, OXAM, XAMO	Water subangle
BRAP...	RAPB, APBR, PBRA	Water subangle
DATT...	ATTD, TTDA, TDAT	Earth subangle
DIOM...	IOMD, OMDI, MDIO	Earth subangle
OOPZ...	OPZO, PZOO, ZOOP	Earth subangle
RGAN...	GANR, ANRG, NRGA	Earth subangle
ADRE...	DREA, READ, EADR	Fire subangle
SISP...	ISPS, SPSI, PSIS	Fire subangle
PALI...	ALIP, LIPA, IPAL	Fire subangle
ACAR...	CARA, ARAC, RACA	Fire subangle

Affixing an appropriate letter from the Tablet of Union to these names also constructs a sort of "super angel." This is not an angel in a leadership position as in the case of the kerubic angel, but rather an angel whose power is much more potent in its effect. These angels have the same nature as the other servient angels, but are much more powerful. It seems implied that these super angels are only to be called in extreme circumstances. I have never called upon them. These angels are called in the same way as the other Servient Angels. They are:

East (Air)

XCZNS	Air subangle
ATOTT	Air subangle
RSIAS	Air subangle
PFMND	Air subangle
XOYVB	Water subangle
APAOC	Water subangle
RRBNH	Water subangle
PDIRI	Water subangle
XABMO	Earth subangle
ANACO	Earth subangle
ROCNM	Earth subangle
PSHAL	Earth subangle
XACCA	Fire subangle
ANPNT	Fire subangle
ROTOI	Fire subangle
PPMOX	Fire subangle

West (Water)

CTOCO	Air subangle
ONHDD	Air subangle
MPAAX	Air subangle
ASAIX	Air subangle
CMAGM	Water subangle
OLEOC	Water subangle
MVSSN	Water subangle
ARVOI	Water subangle
CPACO	Earth subangle
ONDZN	Earth subangle
MIIPO	Earth subangle
AXRNH	Earth subangle
CXPCN	Fire subangle
OVASA	Fire subangle

MDAPI	Fire subangle
ARNIL	Fire subangle

North (Earth)

AAIRA	Air subangle
NORMN	Air subangle
TRSNI	Air subangle
AIZNR	Air subangle
AOMGG	Water subangle
NGBAL	Water subangle
TRLMV	Water subangle
AIAHL	Water subangle
AOPNA	Earth subangle
NDOOP	Earth subangle
TRXAO	Earth subangle
AAXIR	Earth subangle
AMSAP	Fire subangle
NIABA	Fire subangle
TIZXP	Fire subangle
ASTIM	Fire subangle

South (Fire)

IOPMN	Air subangle
TAPST	Air subangle
OSCIO	Air subangle
MVASG	Air subangle
IGMNM	Water subangle
TECOP	Water subangle
OAMOX	Water subangle
MBRAP	Water subangle
IDATT	Earth subangle
TDIOM	Earth subangle
OOOPZ	Earth subangle
MRGAN	Earth subangle
IADRE	Fire subangle
TSISP	Fire subangle

OPALI	Fire subangle
MACAR	Fire subangle

Kakodaimons

There are also "evil" spirit names in these squares. These entities can be used for negative purposes or more material ends. Many people prefer to think of these entities as more "purely elemental," and unintelligent forces rather than evil beings.

Their names are drawn from two letters from below the calvary crosses, beginning with the appropriate letter from the Tablet of Union, thus forming a name of three letters. Dee seems to only derive these names from the left hand side of the cross, but it seems perfectly reasonable to presume that the two letters on the right side equally form a kakodaimonic name. The names could also be theoretically permuted like the kerubic angels, thus forming a very large number of kakodaimons. I will only tabulate the initial forms, as that is an extensive list by itself, and would become quite unmanageable with all of the possible permutations.

These beings are called and constrained by using the calvary cross names backwards.

East (Air)
Air subangle
OGIODI and AZDRA call and control XCZ, XNS, ATO, ATT, RSI, RAS, PFM, PND
Water subangle
AZCALL and MALAP call and control XOY, XVB, APA, AOC, RRB, RNH, PDI, PRI
Earth subangle
IAOAIA and TIIIO call and control XAB, XMO, ANA, ACO, ROC, RNM, PSH, PAL
Fire subangle
ZRRUOA and IAOLA call and control XAC, XCA, ANP, ANT, ROT, ROI, PPM, POX

West (Water)
Air subangle
ATOGBO and OCBAA call and control CTO, CCO, ONH, ODD, MPA, MAX, ASA, AIX
Water subangle
RPALEN and BBEMO call and control CMA, CGM, OLE, OOC, MVS, MSN, ARV, AOI
Earth subangle
IDALAM and DAALO call and control CPA, CCO, OND, OZN, MII, MPO, AXR, ANH
Fire subangle
DSAAAI and APATA call and control CXP, CCN, OVA, OSA, MDA, MPI, ARN, AIL

North (Earth)
Air subangle
IOPGNA and XANNU call and control AAI, ARA, NOR, NMN, TRS, TNI, AIZ, ANR
Water subangle
MEEANA and NDNOS call and control AOM, AGG, NGB, NAL, TRL, TMV, AIA, AHL
Earth subangle
TPLABA and ZIBRA call and control AOP, ANA, NDO, NOP, TRX, TAO, AAX, AIR
Fire subangle
RINMPO and ZIPLI call and control AMS, AAP, NIA, NBA, TIZ, TXP, AST, AIM

South (Fire)
Air subangle
RMLAON and GAOLO call and control IOP, IMN, TAP, TST, OSC, OIO, MVA, MSG
Water subangle
ILADAV and AUABO call and control IGM, INM, TEC, TOP, OAM, OOX, MBR, MAP

Earth subangle
ODXLOU and ADOIS call and control IDA, ITT, TDI, TOM, OOO, OPZ, MRG, MAN
Fire subangle
RNOIZR and MFZRN call and control IAD, IRE, TSI, TSP, OPA, OLI, MAC, MAR

I would recommend that, if you choose to work with these beings at all, you save the communication with these entities for later work rather than earlier. Dee's angels strongly admonished him never to invoke them. I have no practical experience with these beings, and I'm not sure what you can expect from them.

Angels of the Tablet of Union

Finally, from the tablet of union itself, the names of at least nine beings can be extracted. There is no mention of these in any of Dee's writings, but they are frequently called upon by magicians using the Golden Dawn system. These are their names:

EXARP	Air of Spirit
HCOMA	Water of Spirit
NANTA	Earth of Spirit
BITOM	Fire of Spirit
EHNB	Spirit of Spirit
XCAI	Air of Spirit
AONT	Water of Spirit
RMTO	Earth of Spirit
PAAM	Fire of Spirit

Chapter Six
Approaching Enochian Magick from a New Hermetics Perspective

As a New Hermeticist, you have spent a great deal of time and energy analyzing your own nature, creating personal goals, and using consciousness techniques to make changes in your character and experience of the universe. Working with these angels can be an extremely practical expansion of this same process. There are certainly areas in your development that still need more work, and communicating with these intelligent components of universal consciousness can enable you to gain a great deal of transpersonal insight into your own strengths and weaknesses.

You can conduct this work in much the same way that you have approached your earlier work. Look at your goals. Look at your behaviors, emotions, beliefs and drives. In what ways can you seek balance of some manifestation through communication with an intelligence from the Enochian system?

Example: You have trouble getting things accomplished- you feel lazy. *You could invoke the "Mars" senior from the "Earth" Tablet*

Example: you have health problems related to breath. *You could invoke a Servient Angel from "Air" Tablet.*

Example: You are having Financial Troubles. *You could invoke a Kerubic Angel from "Earth of Earth" or the Servient Angel from "Earth of Earth."*

But these examples are really just the very tip of the iceberg. You can also open up dialogues with these beings regarding any area where you are having trouble, both spiritually and practically. In this, be sure to have your inner teacher or connection with your Holy Guardian Angel available to maintain equilibrium.

In asking these angels for advice, the best metaphor I can think of is to conceive of yourself as a young King or Queen. Each of the angels is a sort of tutor, advisor or instructor in the various areas of life, astronomy, diplomacy, mathematics, literature etc., but ultimately the task of ruling your own existence is yours. If you simply follow every piece of advice you are given, you will find yourself going in a thousand different directions and your "country" will fall into ruin. Your work needs to be tempered with reason and balance.

You may also explore the watchtowers in a purely educational light, like a mountain climber or explorer. This is relatively unmapped territory in the collective unconscious or magical universe and you can learn a great deal in this way about the magical universe. This process will be more fully explored in the appendices.

But let's get down to specifics. You must remember that these beings were received by John Dee for the purpose of accomplishing magical goals. They form a system of practical magick for making changes in yourself and your experience of the universe. Many people seem inclined to view work with these angels in entirely spiritual terms, or just as a way to scratch the itch of curiosity. When John Dee received the four watchtowers and learned how to extract the names of the various beings, he quite reasonably asked "but how are they to be used?" His immediate interest was the practical use of these angelic powers, although probably for more intellectual than practical reasons. The answer eventually came.

In Dee's work, the twelve mystical names, the names of the Kings and the names of power from the calvary crosses are merely used as parts of invocations of the other beings. As I said before, many modern magicians have invoked them to conversation, but the purpose for doing so will be up to you, as there is no traditional assignment.

According to Dee's diaries, the 24 seniors all have one purpose, which is "knowledge and judgement in human affairs." This actually fits the use for which most people have put them in modern work. Most magicians go to these angels seeking advice about one thing or another in their lives. In my own work I have often been pleasantly surprised by the accuracy of the information given by these beings, even in predictions for the future. Of course these beings are now associated with various planetary energies thanks to the Golden Dawn.

As for the rest of the names from the watchtowers, the angel Ave gave Dee eight purposes for them within the subquadrants or subangles of the watchtowers:

1. The Secrets of Humanity
2. Medicine and the Cure of Diseases
3. The Knowledge of the Creatures of the Four Elements
4. The Knowledge and Discovery of Metals and Stones
5. The Conjoining and Knitting together of Natures. Destruction of Nature and that which may perish.
6. The Knowledge of Mechanical Crafts, Hand-crafts and Arts
7. Moving from Place to Place
8. Transformation

They are split up amongst the subangles of each watchtower like this:

In the "Air" Subangles (upper left):
The Kerubic Angels- The Conjoining and Knitting together of Natures. Destruction of Nature and that which may perish.
The Servient Angels- Medicine and the Cure of Diseases

In the "Water" Subangles (upper right):
The Kerubic Angels- Moving from Place to Place
The Servient Angels- The Knowledge and Discovery of Metals and Stones

In the "Earth" Subangles (lower left):
The Kerubic Angels- The Knowledge of Mechanical Crafts, Hand-crafts and Arts
The Servient Angels- Transformation

In the "Fire" Subangles (lower right):
The Kerubic Angels- The Secrets of Humanity
The Servient Angels- The Knowledge of the Creatures of the Four Elements

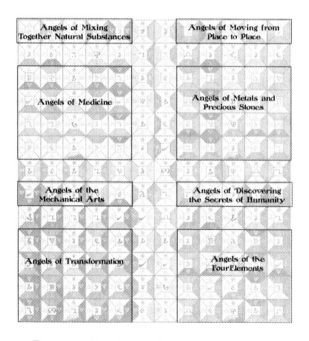

DIAGRAM 11 - ANGEL FUNCTIONS FROM DEE

Each of these purposes applies in all four watchtowers, so that the Kerubic Angels of the "Fire" subquadrants of all four watchtowers, East, West, North and South, all can provide "The

Secrets of Humanity." Again, if you do not view the tablets as elemental, this makes for a somewhat confused situation in which it is fairly unclear why you would invoke any one of them over another.

But it can also be useful to look at them with a more "initiated interpretation." This phrase is most often used in modern times to convert older grimoires into more or less purely psychological terms. While this can have its place in modern magick, it is not entirely what I am suggesting here. What I am proposing is that these beings are, after all, cosmic entities (some might even say trans-cosmic), and the purposes above seem so limited in scope that there is surely something beyond these rather mundane ends within the purview of these beings.

Frater S. A. of the Golden Dawn agreed, and offered some useable reinterpretations, though rather severely garbling the instructions from Dee in some places.

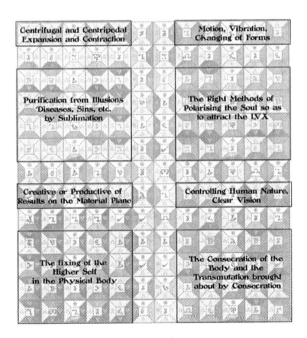

DIAGRAM 12 - GOLDEN DAWN ANGEL FUNCTIONS

But I think looking at these beings through the filter of the elemental comprehensions that you've gained through the New Hermetics will also help you to understand some additional meanings of these angels in a very practical way. Let's take a look at the four elements as they are discussed in a few different places in the New Hermetics.

△   FIRE: warmness and dryness, and the quality of expansion, To Will, Creation, success, passion, lust, creativity, intuition, strength, will, personal power, desire, sexuality, values

▽   WATER: coldness and wetness, and the quality of contraction or shrinking, To Dare, Understanding, friendship, love, tranquility, rest, Relationships, Emotions

△   AIR: warmness and moistness, and the quality of lightness, To Know, Intelligence, education, memory, intellect, teaching, communication, travel, writing, theories, organizing, Beliefs

▽   EARTH: coldness and dryness, and the quality of heaviness, To Keep Silence, Manifestation, money, jobs, promotions, investments, health, business, physical body, construction, physical appearance, Personal Environment, Behaviors

From the above and my personal experiences, I have developed the following expanded interpretations of the functions of these angels. This is merely meant to be suggestive. Your own insights are far more important. Generally, it seems to me that the Kerubic Angels rule over principles, as the source of a particular concept, its archetype so to speak, while the Servient Angels represent the process of the idea as it manifests. You can look at this from a personal or transpersonal perspective- in reality these are one, on different planes of operation.

Transpersonal:

Air subquadrant Kerubic Angels- (knitting together) entropy and negative entropy, centripedal and centrifugal force, order and disorder etc.

Air subquadrant Servient Angels- (medicine) organization and reorganization of systems. The active equilibriation of forces and bodies in the universe

Water subquadrant Kerubic Angels- (moving from place to place) motion and vibration, waveforms and undulation

Water subquadrant Servient Angels- (metals and stones) electromagnetism, gravity, the forces of movement and inertia

Earth subquadrant Kerubic Angels- (mechanical crafts) precipitation, crystallization, and coming together of forms generally

Earth subquadrant Servient Angels- (transformation) processes of digestion, decomposition, solidification

Fire subquadrant Kerubic Angels- (secrets of men) energy and force

Fire subquadrant Servient Angels- (creatures of four elements) life processes- sex, eating, death etc.

Personal:

Air subquadrant Kerubic Angels- (knitting together) beliefs and thinking process

Air subquadrant Servient Angels- (medicine) reorganizing belief systems and thought processes for healing and empowerment

Water subquadrant Kerubic Angels- (moving from place to place) The flow of emotional energy

Water subquadrant Servient Angels- (metals and stones) internal alchemy of emotional release, opening chakras, awakening kundalini etc.

Earth subquadrant Kerubic Angels- (mechanical crafts) Productive behaviors

Earth subquadrant Servient Angels- (transformation) Self Reinvention and personal transformation

Fire subquadrant Kerubic Angels- (secrets of men) Values, passions, drives

Fire subquadrant Servient Angels- (creatures of four elements) using the powers of the four elements to reorient and change inner drives and passions

As you can probably see, the "personal" purposes of these angels correspond very closely with the New Hermetics work in general. This is no accident. However, as I always say, your own interpretation and practical experience in these matters is more important than any convenient scheme that I have created.

But in this interpretation, these angels are the intelligences behind the cosmic forces that create reality, as well as powers that operate in us microcosmically as the forces of personality and experience. But this latter should in no way give you the impression that I view these beings as "merely" subjective. In working with these beings I have had experiences seeing spirits with my physical eyes, causing wind and rain, receiving correct answers and prophecies and generally experiencing enough macrocosmic confirmation of their existence to convince most people with a normal, healthy skepticism. But I still hold tend to hold that these beings are subjective to a certain degree as well. I do this because it can be just as dangerous to believe in or to disbelieve in spirits. As a magician you must understand that belief is as much a tool in your arsenal as your sword. Use it wisely. I think the greatest danger in working with entities is that we give them too much objective existence and begin to worship them as false gods. Don't fall into this trap. Maintain your sovereignty in both your inner and outer world. Bend your knee to no one, human or divine. Equally, do not force these angels to merely be fantasies from your subconcsious. They can connect you with a vast hierarchy of consciousness and being beyond the boundaries of your internal personal experience.

It is interesting to note that the two reinterpretations I suggest can really represent two poles, from the extreme of objectivity to the extreme of subjectivity, with the traditional meaning assigned by Dee operating somewhere in the middle. Of course it should be noted the "poles" described above are by no means the end of possible interpretations which could extend into spiritual places far beyond personal issues or physical phenomena.

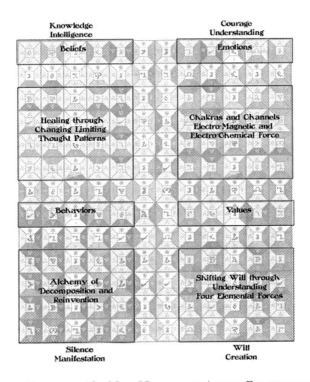

DIAGRAM 13 - NEW HERMETICS ANGEL FUNCTIONS

There is one last issue to discuss before moving into the protocols for conjuration. The Golden Dawn took the elemental attributions within the watchtowers one step further, assigning a pyramid of elemental attributions (as well as astrological and Qabalistic) to each letter square. While I won't go deeply into the manner in which these assignments were made, basically it has to do with permutations of the Tetragrammaton, YHVH, whose letters are assigned to the four elements. So each square can actually be viewed as having four elemental attributions. Since the nature of each angel is determined by the first letter of their name, this makes for more nuanced differences in the character of the angels. For instance, while RZLA and ARZL are both Kerubic angels in the air subquadrant of the air tablet of the east, RZLA is dominated by air, while ARZL also has some earth influence. This may be useful to you in determining exactly which angel you wish to work with. For this reason the charts that follow include the pyramids of the letters, although they may be a bit small for reading out of this book. Color renditions of these tablets are available in the companion volume to this book *The Enochian Conjuration Workbook*. I have also noted some of these elemental distinctions where it is practical. You do not need to understand this fully in order to proceed with Enochian magick in general. This is a very speculative Golden Dawn addition.

The following pages form a convenient "grimoire," offering the names of each of the beings in the four watchtowers, along with the procedure for calling them forth. It should be remembered that while the procedure for calling these spirits forth is mechanical and digital, the actual experience of doing so is fluid and analog. This is much more akin to an art than a science, though neither accurately describe the process at all. You are on the one hand actively creating the correct atmosphere inwardly and outwardly with your temple and ritual devices, but you are also calling upon ineffable mystery of the magical realm, and hoping to leap down the rabbit hole into the unknown. Jump in.

King of the Air Tablet

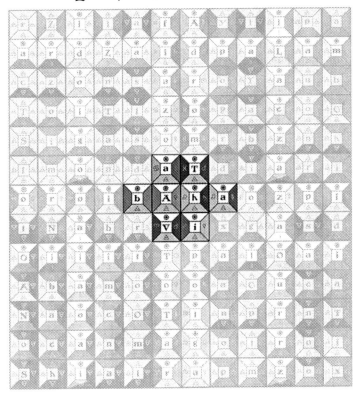

BATAIVAH

Purpose: Rulership of the Air Tablet, or issues relating to a combination of Solar and airy energies.

Procedure:

1. Air Temple opening
2. Third Enochian Key
3. Vibrate: Three Names of God (ORO IBAH AOZPI), Elemental King (BATAIVAH)

Seniors of the Air Tablet

HIPOTGA	Saturn
AAOZAIF	Jupiter
HABIORO	Mars
AHAOZPI	Venus
AVTOTAR	Mercury
HTMORDA	Moon

Purpose: Knowledge and Judgement in human affairs, or issues relating to a combination of planetary and airy energies.

Procedure:

1. Air Temple opening
2. Third Enochian Key
3. Vibrate: Three Names of God (ORO IBAH AOZPI), Elemental King (BATAIVAH), Senior's name (with appropriate planetary hexagram)

Kerubic Archangel
Air of Air

ERZLA

Purpose: Leading the Kerubic Angels

Procedure:

1. Air Temple opening
2. Third Enochian Key
3. Vibrate: Three Names of God (ORO IBAH AOZPI), Elemental King (BATAIVAH), Archangel's name (ERZLA)

Kerubic Angels
Air of Air

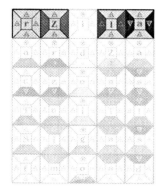

RZLA	-	Air dominance
ZLAR	-	Water influence
LARZ	-	Fire influence
ARZL	-	Earth influence

Purpose: Mixing together natural substances. Entropy and Negative Entropy, centripedal and centrifugal force, Order and Disorder etc. Beliefs and Thinking Process.

Procedure:

1. Air Temple opening
2. Third Enochian Key
3. Vibrate: Three Names of God (ORO IBAH AOZPI), Elemental King (BATAIVAH), Kerubic Archangel (ERZLA), Kerubic Angel's name

Servient Angels
Air of Air

CZNS - Earth influence
TOTT - Fire influence
SIAS - Water influence
FMND - Air dominance

(other permutations are also possible)

Purpose: Medicine and the Cure of Diseases. Organization and reorganization of systems. The active equilibriation of forces and bodies in the universe. Reorganizing belief systems and thought processes for healing and empowerment.

Procedure:

1. Air Temple opening
2. Third Enochian Key
3. Vibrate: Three Names of God (ORO IBAH AOZPI), Elemental King (BATAIVAH), Six-lettered name to conjure (IDOIGO), Five-lettered Name to control (ARDZA), Servient Angel's name

Kakodaimons
Air of Air

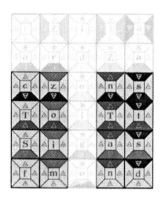

XCZ, XNS	- Earth influence
ATO, ATT	- Fire influence
RSI, RAS	- Water influence
PFM, PND	- Air dominance

(other permutations are also possible)

Purpose: Poisoning and Causing Diseases

Procedure:

1. Air Temple opening
2. Third Enochian Key
3. Vibrate: Three Names of God (ORO IBAH AOZPI), Elemental King (BATAIVAH), Six-lettered Name to conjure (OGIODI), Five-lettered Name to control (AZDRA), Kakodaimon's name

Kerubic Archangel
Water of Air

EYTPA

Purposes: Leading Kerubic Angels

Procedure:

1. Air Temple opening
2. Third Enochian Key
3. Seventh Enochian Key
4. Vibrate: Three Names of God (ORO IBAH AOZPI), Elemental King (BATAIVAH), Archangel's name (EYTPA)

ꝁerubíc Angelſ
Water of Aír

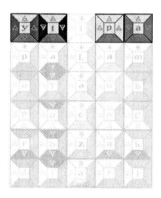

YTPA	-	Fire influence
TPAY	-	Earth influence
PAYT	-	Air dominance
AYPT	-	Water dominance

Purposes: Mixing together natural substances. Motion and vibration, waveforms and undulation. The flow of emotional energy.

Procedure

1. Air Temple opening
2. Third Enochian Key
3. Seventh Enochian Key
4. Three Names of God (ORO IBAH AOZPI), Elemental King (BATAIVAH), Archangel's name (EYTPA), Kerubic Angel's name

80

Servient Angels
Water of Air

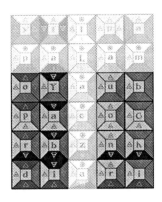

OYUB -	Water dominance
PAOC -	Air dominance
RBNH -	Earth influence
DIRI -	Fire influence

(other permutations are also possible)

Purpose: The Knowledge and discovery of metals and stones. Electromagnetism, gravity, the forces of movement and inertia. Internal alchemy of emotional release, opening chakras, awakening kundalini etc.

Procedure:

1. Air Temple opening
2. Third Enochian Key
3. Vibrate: Three Names of God (ORO IBAH AOZPI), Elemental King (BATAIVAH), Six-lettered Name to conjure (LLACZA), Five-lettered Name to control (PALAM), Servient Angel's name

Kakodaimons
Water of Air

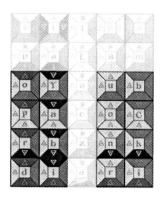

XOY, XUB	- Water dominance
APA, AOC	- Air dominance
RRB, RNH	- Earth influence
PDI, PRI	- Fire influence

(other permutations are also possible)

Purposes: Obtaining coined metal (Concealing Metals and Stones?)

Procedure:

1. Air Temple opening
2. Third Enochian Key
3. Vibrate: Three Names of God (ORO IBAH AOZPI), Elemental King (BATAIVAH), Six-lettered Name to conjure (AZCALL), Five-lettered Name to control (MALAP), Kakodaimon's name.

Kerubic Archangel Earth of Air

ETNBR

Purposes: Leading Kerubic Angels

Procedure:

1. Air Temple opening
2. Third Enochian Key
3. Eighth Enochian Key
4. Vibrate: Three Names of God (ORO IBAH AOZPI), Elemental King (BATAIVAH), Archangel's name (ETNBR)

Kerubic Angels
Earth of Air

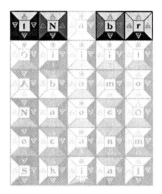

TNBR -	Earth dominance
NBRT -	Fire influence
BRTN -	Water influence
RTNB -	Air dominance

Purposes: The knowledge of mechanical crafts, hand-crafts and arts. Precipitation, crystallization, and coming together of forms generally. Productive behaviors.

Procedure:

1. Air Temple opening
2. Third Enochian Key
3. Eighth Enochian Key
4. Three Names of God (ORO IBAH AOZPI), Elemental King (BATAIVAH), Archangel's name (ETNBR), Kerubic Angel's name

Servient Angels
Earth of Air

ABMO -	Air dominance
NACO -	Water influence
OCNM-	Fire influence
SHAL -	Earth dominance

(other permutations are also possible)

Purpose: Transformation. Processes of digestion, decomposition, solidification. Self Reinvention and personal transformation

Procedure:

1. Air Temple opening
2. Third Enochian Key
3. Eighth Enochian Key
4. Vibrate: Three Names of God (ORO IBAH AOZPI), Elemental King (BATAIVAH), Six-lettered Name to conjure (AIAOAI), Five-lettered Name to control (OIIIT), Servient Angel's name

Kakodaimons
Earth of Air

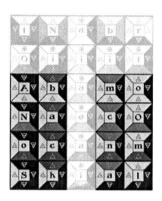

XAB, XMO	- Air dominance
ANA, ACO	- Water influence
ROC, RNM	- Fire influence
PSH, PAL	- Earth dominance

(other permutations are also possible)

Purposes: (Destruction? Dissolution?)

Procedure:

1. Air Temple opening
2. Third Enochian Key
3. Eighth Enochian Key
4. Vibrate: Three Names of God (ORO IBAH AOZPI), Elemental King (BATAIVAH), Six-lettered Name to conjure (IAOAIA), Five-lettered Name to control (TIIIO), Kakodaimon's name

Kerubic Archangel
Fire of Air

EXGSD

Purposes: Leading Kerubic Angels

Procedure:

1. Air Temple opening
2. Third Enochian Key
3. Ninth Enochian Key
4. Vibrate: Three Names of God (ORO IBAH AOZPI), Elemental King (BATAIVAH), Archangel's name (EXGSD)

Kerubic Angels
Fire of Air

XGSD -   Water influence
GSDX -   Air dominance
SDXG -   Earth influence
DXGS -   Fire dominance

Purposes: The Secrets of Humanity. Energy and force. Values, passions, drives

Procedure:

1. Air Temple opening
2. Third Enochian Key
3. Ninth Enochian Key
4. Three Names of God (ORO IBAH AOZPI), Elemental King (BATAIVAH), Archangel's name (EXGSD), Kerubic Angel's name

Servient Angels
Fire of Air

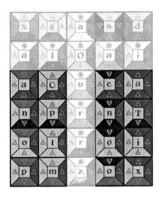

ACCA -	Fire dominance
NPNT -	Earth influence
OTOI -	Air dominance
PMOX -	Water Influence

(other permutations are also possible)

Purpose: The Knowledge of the creatures of the four elements. Life processes- sex, eating, death etc. Using the powers of the four elements to reorient and change inner drives and passions

Procedure:

1. Air Temple opening
2. Third Enochian key
3. Ninth Enochian key
4. Vibrate: Three Names of God (ORO IBAH AOZPI), Elemental King (BATAIVAH), Six-lettered Name to conjure (AOURRZ), Five-lettered Name to control (ALOAI), Servient Angel's name

Kakodaimons
Fire of Air

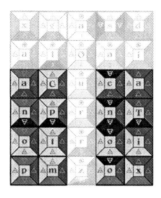

XAC, XCA	- Fire dominance
ANP, ANT	- Earth influence
ROT, ROI	- Air dominance
PPM, POX	- Water influence

(other permutations are also possible)

Purposes: (Negative or destructive use of the four elements?)

Procedure:

1. Air Temple opening
2. Third Enochian Key
3. Ninth Enochian Key
4. Vibrate: Three Names of God (ORO IBAH AOZPI), Elemental King (BATAIVAH), Six-lettered Name to conjure (ZRRUOA), Five-lettered Name to control (IAOLA), Kakodaimon's name

King of the Water Tablet

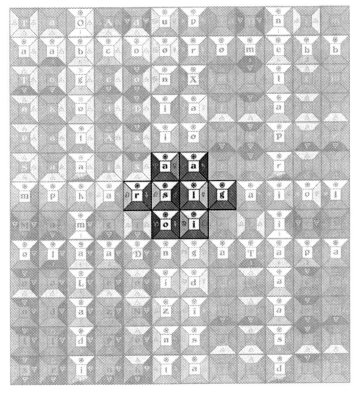

RAAGIOSL

Purpose: Rulership of the Water Tablet, or issues relating to a combination of Solar and watery energies.

Procedure:

1. Water Temple opening
2. Fourth Enochian Key
3. Vibrate: Three Names of God (MPH ARSL GAIOL), Elemental King (RAAGIOSL)

Seniors of the Water Tablet

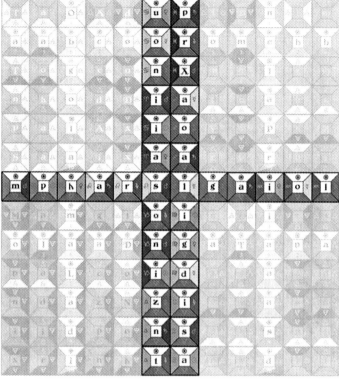

LIGDISA	Saturn
SAIINOV	Jupiter
LSRAHPM	Mars
SLGAIOL	Venus
SONIZNT	Mercury
LAOAXRP	Moon

Purpose: Knowledge and Judgement in human affairs, or issues relating to a combination of planetary and watery energies.

Procedure:

1. Water Temple opening
2. Fourth Enochian Key
3. Vibrate: Three Names of God (MPH ARSL GAIOL), Elemental King (RAAGIOSL), Name of Senior (with appropriate planetary hexagram)

Kerubic Archangel
Air of Water

HTAAD

Purpose: Leading the Kerubic Angels

Procedure:

1. Water Temple opening
2. Fourth Enochian Key
3. Tenth Enochian Key
4. Vibrate: Three Names of God (MPH ARSL GAIOL), Elemental King (RAAGIOSL), Archangel's name (HTAAD)

ßerubic Angels
Air of Water

TAAD -	Air dominates
AADT -	Water influence
ADTA -	Fire influence
DTAA -	Earth influence

Purpose: Mixing together natural substances. Entropy and Negative Entropy, centripedal and centrifugal force, Order and Disorder etc. Beliefs and Thinking Process.

Procedure:

1. Water Temple opening
2. Fourth Enochian Key
3. Tenth Enochian Key
4. Vibrate: Three Names of God (MPH ARSL GAIOL), Elemental King (RAAGIOSL), Archangel's name (HTAAD), Kerubic Angel's name

Servient Angels
Air of Water

TOCO -	Earth Influence
NHDD-	Fire influence
PAAX -	Water dominance
SAIX -	Air dominance

(other permutations are also possible)

Purpose: Medicine and the Cure of Diseases. Organization and reorganization of systems. The active equilibriation of forces and bodies in the universe. Reorganizing belief systems and thought processes for healing and empowerment.

Procedure:

1. Water Temple opening
2. Fourth Enochian Key
3. Tenth Enochian Key
4. Vibrate: Three Names of God (MPH ARSL GAIOL), Elemental King (RAAGIOSL), Six-lettered name to conjure (OBGOTA), Five-lettered Name to control (AABCO), Servient Angel's name

Kakodaimons
Air of Water

CTO, CCO	- Earth Influence
ONH, ODD	- Fire influence
MPA, MAX	- Water influence
ASA, AIX	- Air dominance

(other permutations are also possible)

Purpose: Poisoning and Causing Diseases

Procedure:

1. Water Temple opening
2. Fourth Enochian Key
3. Tenth Enochian Key
4. Vibrate: Three Names of God (MPH ARSL GAIOL), Elemental King (RAAGIOSL), Six-lettered name to conjure (ATOGBO), Five-lettered Name to control (OCBAA), Kakodaimon's name

ʃerubíc Archangeʃ
Water of Water

HTDIM

Purposes: Leading Kerubic Angels

Procedure:

1. Water Temple opening
2. Fourth Enochian Key
3. Vibrate: Three Names of God (MPH ARSL GAIOL), Elemental King (RAAGIOSL), Archangel's name (HTDIM)

Kerubic Angels
Water of Water

TDIM -	Fire influence
TPAY -	Earth influence
PAYT -	Air influence
AYPT -	Water dominance

Purposes: Mixing together natural substances. Motion and vibration, waveforms and undulation. The flow of emotional energy.

Procedure

1. Water Temple opening
2. Fourth Enochian Key
3. Vibrate: Three Names of God (MPH ARSL GAIOL), Elemental King (RAAGIOSL), Archangel's name (HTDIM), Kerubic Angel's name

Servient Angels
Water of Water

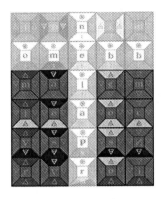

MAGM-	Water Dominance
LEOC -	Air influence
VSSN -	Earth influence
RVOI -	Fire influence

(other permutations are also possible)

Purpose: The Knowledge and discovery of metals and stones. Electromagnetism, gravity, the forces of movement and inertia. Internal alchemy of emotional release, opening chakras, awakening kundalini etc.

Procedure:

1. Water Temple opening
2. Fourth Enochian Key
3. Vibrate: Three Names of God (MPH ARSL GAIOL), Elemental King (RAAGIOSL), Six-lettered name to conjure (NELAPR), Five-lettered Name to control (OMEBB), Servient Angel's name

Kakodaimons
Water of Water

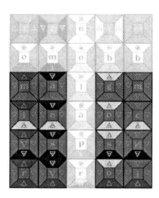

CMA, CGM	- Water dominance
OLE, OOC	- Air influence
MVC, MSN	- Earth influence
ARV, AOI	- Fire influence

(other permutations are also possible)

Purposes: Obtaining coined metal (Concealing Metals and Stones?)

Procedure:

1. Water Temple opening
2. Fourth Enochian Key
3. Vibrate: Three Names of God (MPH ARSL GAIOL), Elemental King (RAAGIOSL), Six-lettered name to conjure (RPALEN), Five-lettered Name to control (BBEMO), Kakodaimon's name.

Kerubic Archangel
Earth of Water

HMAGL

Purposes: Leading Kerubic Angels

Procedure:

1. Water Temple opening
2. Fourth Enochian Key
3. Eleventh Enochian Key
4. Vibrate: Three Names of God (MPH ARSL GAIOL), Elemental King (RAAGIOSL), Archangel's name (HMAGL)

Kerubic Angels
Earth of Water

MAGL -	Earth dominance
AGLM -	Fire influence
GLMA -	Water influence
LMAG -	Air influence

Purposes: The knowledge of mechanical crafts, hand-crafts and arts. Precipitation, crystallization, and coming together of forms generally. Productive behaviors.

Procedure:

1. Water Temple opening
2. Fourth Enochian Key
3. Eleventh Enochian Key
4. Vibrate: Three Names of God (MPH ARSL GAIOL), Elemental King (RAAGIOSL), Archangel's name (HMAGL), Kerubic Angel's name

Servient Angels
Earth of Water

PACO -	Air influence
NDZN -	Water dominance
IIPO -	Fire influence
XRNH -	Earth dominance

(other permutations are also possible)

Purpose: Transformation. Processes of digestion, decomposition, solidification. Self Reinvention and personal transformation

Procedure:

1. Water Temple opening
2. Fourth Enochian Key
3. Eleventh Enochian Key
4. Vibrate: Three Names of God (MPH ARSL GAIOL), Elemental King (RAAGIOSL), Six-lettered name to conjure (MALADI), Five-lettered Name to control (OLAAD), Servient Angel's name

Kakodaimons
Earth of Water

CPA, CCO — Air influence
OND, OZN — Water dominance
MII, MPO — Fire influence
AXR, ANH — Earth dominance

(other permutations are also possible)

Purposes: (Destruction? Dissolution?)

Procedure:

1. Water Temple opening
2. Fourth Enochian Key
3. Eleventh Enochian Key
4. Vibrate: Three Names of God (MPH ARSL GAIOL), Elemental King (RAAGIOSL), Six-lettered name to conjure (IDALAM), Five-lettered Name to control (DAALO), Kakodaimon's name

Kerubic Archangel
Fire of Water

HNLRX

Purposes: Leading Kerubic Angels

Procedure:

1. Water Temple opening
2. Fourth Enochian Key
3. Twelfth Enochian Key
4. Vibrate: Three Names of God (MPH ARSL GAIOL), Elemental King (RAAGIOSL), Archangel's name (HNLRX)

Kerubic Angels
Fire of Water

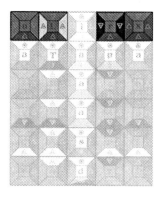

NLRX -	Water dominance
LRXN -	Air influence
RXNL -	Earth influence
XNLR -	Fire dominance

Purposes: The Secrets of Humanity. Energy and force. Values, passions, drives

Procedure:

1. Water Temple opening
2. Fourth Enochian Key
3. Twelfth Enochian Key
4. Vibrate: Three Names of God (MPH ARSL GAIOL), Elemental King (RAAGIOSL), Archangel's name (HNLRX), Kerubic Angel's name

Servient Angels
Fire of Water

XPCN -	Fire dominance
VASA -	Earth influence
DAPI -	Air influence
RNIL -	Water dominance

(other permutations are also possible)

Purpose: The Knowledge of the creatures of the four elements. Life processes- sex, eating, death etc. Using the powers of the four elements to reorient and change inner drives and passions

Procedure:

1. Water Temple opening
2. Fourth Enochian Key
3. Twelfth Enochian Key
4. Vibrate: Three Names of God (MPH ARSL GAIOL), Elemental King (RAAGIOSL), Six-lettered Name to conjure (IAAASD), Five-lettered Name to control (ATAPA), Servient Angel's name

Kakodaimons Fire of Water

CXP, CCN	- Fire dominance
OVA, OSA	- Earth influence
MDA, MPI	- Air influence
ARN, AIL	- Water dominance

(other permutations are also possible)

Purposes: (Negative or destructive use of the four elements?)

Procedure:

1. Water Temple opening
2. Fourth Enochian Key
3. Twelfth Enochian Key
4. Vibrate: Three Names of God (MPH ARSL GAIOL), Elemental King (RAAGIOSL), Six-lettered Name to conjure (DSAAAI), Five-lettered Name to control (APATA), Kakodaimon's name

King of the Earth Tablet

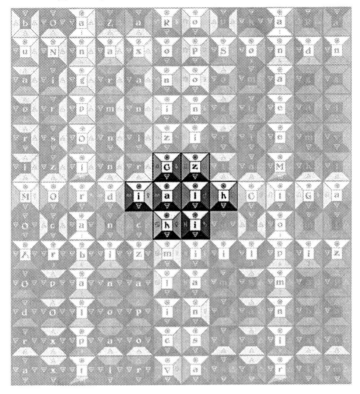

ICZHIHAL

Purpose: Rulership of the Earth Tablet, or issues relating to a combination of Solar and earthy energies.

Procedure:

1. Earth Temple opening
2. Fifth Enochian Key
3. Vibrate: Three Names of God (MOR DIAL HCTGA), Elemental King (ICZHIHAL)

Seniors of the Earth Tablet

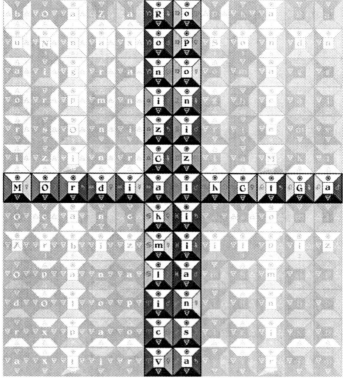

LIIANSA	Saturn
ACZINOR	Jupiter
LAIDROM	Mars
ALHCTGA	Venus
AHMLICV	Mercury
LZINOPO	Moon

Purpose: Knowledge and Judgement in human affairs, or issues relating to a combination of planetary and earthy energies.

Procedure:

1. Earth Temple opening
2. Fifth Enochian Key
3. Vibrate: Three Names of God (MOR DIAL HCTGA), Elemental King (ICZHIHAL), Senior's name (with appropriate planetary hexagram)

Kerubic Archangel
Air of Earth

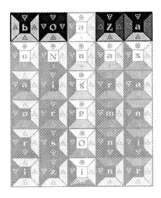

NBOZA

Purpose: Leading the Kerubic Angels

Procedure:

1. Earth Temple opening
2. Fifth Enochian Key
3. Thirteenth Enochian Key
4. Vibrate: Three Names of God (MOR DIAL HCTGA), Elemental King (ICZHIHAL), Archangel's name (NBOZA)

Kerubic Angels
Air of Earth

BOZA -   Air dominates
OZAB -   Earth dominates
ZABO -   Fire influence
ABOZ -   Water influence

Purpose: Mixing together natural substances. Entropy and Negative Entropy, centripedal and centrifugal force, Order and Disorder etc. Beliefs and Thinking Process.

Procedure:

1. Earth Temple opening
2. Fifth Enochian Key
3. Thirteenth Enochian Key
4. Vibrate: Three Names of God (MOR DIAL HCTGA), Elemental King (ICZHIHAL), Archangel's name (NBOZA), Kerubic Angel's name

Servient Angels
Air of Earth

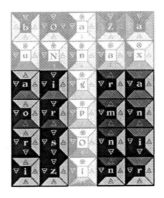

AIRA -	Water influence
ORMN-	Fire influence
RSNI -	Earth dominance
IZNR -	Air dominance

(other permutations are also possible)

Purpose: Medicine and the Cure of Diseases. Organization and reorganization of systems. The active equilibriation of forces and bodies in the universe. Reorganizing belief systems and thought processes for healing and empowerment.

Procedure:

1. Earth Temple opening
2. Fifth Enochian Key
3. Thirteenth Enochian Key
4. Vibrate: Three Names of God (MOR DIAL HCTGA), Elemental King (ICZHIHAL), Six-lettered name to conjure (ANGPOI), Five-lettered Name to control (UNNAX), Servient Angel's name

Kakodaimons
Air of Earth

AAI, ARA	- Water influence
NOR, NMN	- Fire influence
TRS, TNI	- Earth dominance
AIZ, ANR	- Air dominance

(other permutations are also possible)

Purpose: Poisoning and Causing Diseases

Procedure:

1. Earth Temple opening
2. Fifth Enochian Key
3. Thirteenth Enochian Key
4. Vibrate: Three Names of God (MOR DIAL HCTGA), Elemental King (ICZHIHAL), Six-lettered name to conjure (IOPGNA), Five-lettered Name to control (XANNU), Kakodaimon's name

Kerubic Archangel Water of Earth

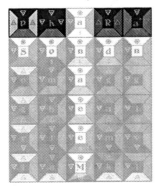

NPHRA

Purposes: Leading Kerubic Angels

Procedure:

1. Earth Temple opening
2. Fifth Enochian Key
3. Fourteenth Enochian Key
4. Vibrate: Three Names of God (MOR DIAL HCTGA), Elemental King (ICZHIHAL), Archangel's name (NPHRA)

Kerubic Angels
Water of Earth

PHRA -	Air influence
HRAP -	Earth dominance
RAPH -	Fire influence
APHR -	Water dominance

Purposes: Mixing together natural substances. Motion and vibration, waveforms and undulation. The flow of emotional energy.

Procedure:

1. Earth Temple opening
2. Fifth Enochian Key
3. Fourteenth Enochian Key
4. Vibrate: Three Names of God (MOR DIAL HCTGA), Elemental King (ICZHIHAL), Archangel's name (NPHRA), Kerubic Angel's name

Servient Angels
Water of Earth

OMGG-	Water dominance
GBAL -	Fire influence
RLMV -	Earth dominance
IAHL -	Air influence

(other permutations are also possible)

Purpose: The Knowledge and discovery of metals and stones. Electromagnetism, gravity, the forces of movement and inertia. Internal alchemy of emotional release, opening chakras, awakening kundalini etc.

Procedure:

1. Earth Temple opening
2. Fifth Enochian Key
3. Fourteenth Enochian Key
4. Vibrate: Three Names of God (MOR DIAL HCTGA), Elemental King (ICZHIHAL), Six-lettered Name to conjure (ANAEEM), Five-lettered Name to control (SONDN), Servient Angel's name

Kakodaimons
Water of Earth

AOM, AGG	- Water dominance
NGB, NAL	- Fire influence
TRL, TMV	- Earth dominance
AIA, AHL	- Air influence

(other permutations are also possible)

Purposes: Obtaining coined metal (Concealing Metals and Stones?)

Procedure:

1. Earth Temple opening
2. Fifth Enochian Key
3. Fourteenth Enochian Key
4. Vibrate: Three Names of God (MOR DIAL HCTGA), Elemental King (ICZHIHAL), Six-lettered Name to conjure (MEEANA), Five-lettered Name to control (NDNOS), Kakodaimon's name.

Kerubic Archangel Earth of Earth

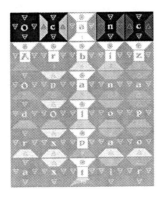

NOCNC

Purposes: Leading Kerubic Angels

Procedure:

1. Earth Temple opening
2. Fifth Enochian Key
3. Vibrate: Three Names of God (MOR DIAL HCTGA), Elemental King (ICZHIHAL), Archangel's name (NOCNC)

Kerubic Angels
Earth of Earth

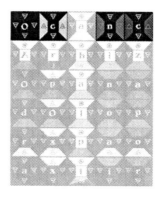

OCNC - Earth dominance
CNCO - Air influence
NCOC - Water influence
COCN - Fire influence

Purposes: The knowledge of mechanical crafts, hand-crafts and arts. Precipitation, crystallization, and coming together of forms generally. Productive behaviors.

Procedure:

1. Earth Temple opening
2. Fifth Enochian Key
3. Vibrate: Three Names of God (MOR DIAL HCTGA), Elemental King (ICZHIHAL), Archangel's name (NOCNC), Kerubic Angel's name

Servient Angels
Earth of Earth

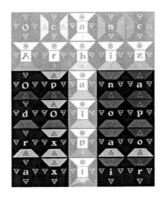

OPNA -	Fire influence
DOOP -	Water influence
RXAO -	Air influence
AXIR -	Earth dominance

(other permutations are also possible)

Purpose: Transformation. Processes of digestion, decomposition, solidification. Self Reinvention and personal transformation

Procedure:

1. Earth Temple opening
2. Fifth Enochian Key
3. Vibrate: Three Names of God (MOR DIAL HCTGA), Elemental King (ICZHIHAL), Six-lettered Name to conjure (ABALPT), Five-lettered Name to control (ARBIZ), Servient Angel's name

ꝁakoδaimons
Earth of Earth

AOP, ANA	- Fire influence
NDO, NOP	- Water influence
TRX, TAO	- Air influence
AAX, AIR	- Earth dominance

(other permutations are also possible)

Purposes: (Destruction? Dissolution?)

Procedure:

1. Earth Temple opening
2. Fifth Enochian Key
3. Vibrate: Three Names of God (MOR DIAL HCTGA), Elemental King (ICZHIHAL), Six-lettered Name to conjure (TPLABA), Five-lettered Name to control (ZIBRA), Servient Angel's nameKakodaimon's name

Kerubic Archangel
Fire of Earth

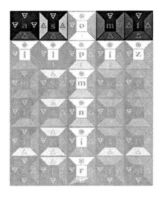

NASMT

Purposes: Leading Kerubic Angels

Procedure:

1. Earth Temple opening
2. Fifth Enochian Key
3. Fifteenth Enochian Key
4. Vibrate: Three Names of God (MOR DIAL HCTGA), Elemental King (ICZHIHAL), Archangel's name (NASMT)

Kerubic Angels Fire of Earth

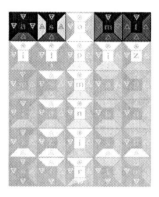

ASMT -   Earth dominance
SMTA -   Air influence
MTAS -   Water influence
TASM -   Fire dominance

Purposes: The Secrets of Humanity. Energy and force. Values, passions, drives

Procedure

1. Earth Temple opening
2. Fifth Enochian Key
3. Fifteenth Enochian Key
4. Vibrate: Three Names of God (MOR DIAL HCTGA), Elemental King (ICZHIHAL), Archangel's name (NASMT), Kerubic Angel's name

Servient Angels
Fire of Earth

MSAP -	Fire dominance	
IABA -	Water influence	
IZXP -	Air influence	
STIM -	Earth dominance	

(other permutations are also possible)

Purpose: The Knowledge of the creatures of the four elements. Life processes- sex, eating, death etc. Using the powers of the four elements to reorient and change inner drives and passions

Procedure:

1. Earth Temple opening
2. Fifth Enochian Key
3. Fifteenth Enochian Key
4. Vibrate: Three Names of God (MOR DIAL HCTGA), Elemental King (ICZHIHAL), Six-lettered Name to conjure (OPMNIR), Five-lettered Name to control (ILPIZ), Servient Angel's name

Kakodaimons
Fire of Earth

AMS, AAP	- Fire dominance
NIA, NBA	- Water influence
TIZ, TXP	- Air influence
AST, AIM	- Earth dominance

(other permutations are also possible)

Purposes: (Negative or destructive use of the four elements?)

Procedure:

1. Earth Temple opening
2. Fifth Enochian Key
3. Fifteenth Enochian Key
4. Vibrate: Three Names of God (MOR DIAL HCTGA), Elemental King (ICZHIHAL), Six-lettered Name to conjure (RINMPO), Five-lettered Name to control (ZIPLI), Kakodaimon's name

126

King of the Fire Tablet

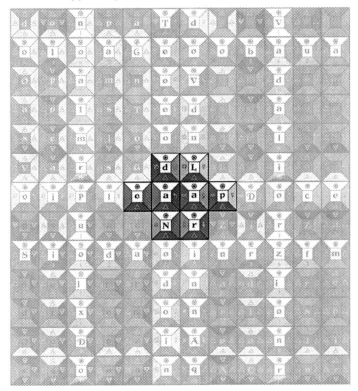

EDLPRNAA

Purpose: Rulership of the Fire Tablet, or issues relating to a combination of Solar and fiery energies.

Procedure:

1. Fire Temple opening
2. Sixth Enochian Key
3. Vibrate: Three Names of God (OIP TEAA PDOCE), Elemental King (EDLPRNAA)

Seniors of the Fire Tablet

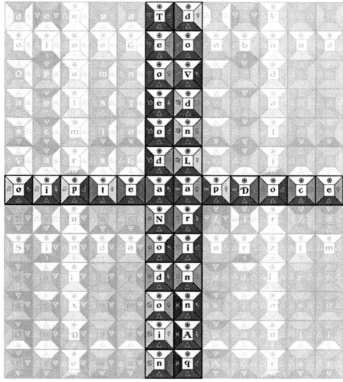

ARINNAP	Saturn
ADOEOET	Jupiter
AAETPIO	Mars
AAPDOCE	Venus
ANODOIN	Mercury
ALNDVOD	Moon

Purpose: Knowledge and Judgement in human affairs, or issues relating to a combination of planetary and fiery energies.

Procedure:

1. Fire Temple opening
2. Sixth Enochian Key
3. Vibrate: Three Names of God (OIP TEAA PDOCE), Elemental King (EDLPRNAA), Senior's name (with appropriate planetary hexagram)

Kerubic Archangel
Air of Fire

BDOPA

Purpose: Leading the Kerubic Angels

Procedure:

1. Fire Temple opening
2. Sixth Enochian Key
3. Sixteenth Enochian Key
4. Vibrate: Three Names of God (OIP TEAA PDOCE), Elemental King (EDLPRNAA), Archangel's name (BDOPA)

Kerubic Angels
Air of Fire

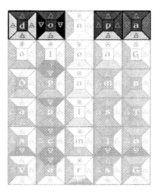

DOPA -	Air dominates
OPAD -	Earth influence
PADO -	Fire dominates
ADOP -	Water influence

Purpose: Mixing together natural substances. Entropy and Negative Entropy, centripedal and centrifugal force, Order and Disorder etc. Beliefs and Thinking Process.

Procedure:

1. Fire Temple opening
2. Sixth Enochian Key
3. Sixteenth Enochian Key
4. Vibrate: Three Names of God (OIP TEAA PDOCE), Elemental King (EDLPRNAA), Archangel's name (BDOPA), Kerubic Angel's name

Servient Angels
Air of Fire

OPAM	-	Water influence
APST	-	Fire dominance
SCIO	-	Earth influence
VASG	-	Air dominance

(other permutations are also possible)

Purpose: Medicine and the Cure of Diseases. Organization and reorganization of systems. The active equilibration of forces and bodies in the universe. Reorganizing belief systems and thought processes for healing and empowerment.

Procedure:

1. Fire Temple opening
2. Sixth Enochian Key
3. Sixteenth Enochian Key
4. Vibrate: Three Names of God (OIP TEAA PDOCE), Elemental King (EDLPRNAA), Six-lettered name to conjure (NOALMR), Five-lettered Name to control (OLOAG), Servient Angel's name

Kakodaimons
Air of Fire

IOP, IAM	- Water influence
TAP, TST	- Fire dominance
OSC, OIO	- Earth influence
MVA, MSG	- Air dominance

(other permutations are also possible)

Purpose: Poisoning and Causing Diseases

Procedure:

1. Fire Temple opening
2. Sixth Enochian Key
3. Sixteenth Enochian Key
4. Vibrate: Three Names of God (OIP TEAA PDOCE), Elemental King (EDLPRNAA), Six-lettered name to conjure (RMLAON), Five-lettered Name to control (GAOLO), Kakodaimon's name

Kerubic Archangel Water of Fire

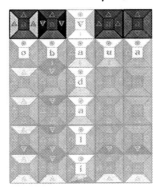

BANAA

Purposes: Leading Kerubic Angels

Procedure:

1. Fire Temple opening
2. Sixth Enochian Key
3. Seventeenth Enochian Key
4. Vibrate: Three Names of God (OIP TEAA PDOCE), Elemental King (EDLPRNAA), Archangel's name (BANAA)

Kerubic Angels
Water of Fire

ANAA-	Air influence
NAAA-	Earth influence
AAAN-	Fire dominance
AANA-	Water dominance

Purposes: Mixing together natural substances. Motion and vibration, waveforms and undulation. The flow of emotional energy.

Procedure:

1. Fire Temple opening
2. Sixth Enochian Key
3. Seventeenth Enochian Key
4. Vibrate: Three Names of God (OIP TEAA PDOCE), Elemental King (EDLPRNAA), Archangel's name (BANAA), Kerubic Angel's name

Servient Angels
Water of fire

GMNM-	Water dominance
ECOP -	Fire dominance
AMOX-	Earth influence
BRAP -	Air influence

(other permutations are also possible)

Purpose: The Knowledge and discovery of metals and stones. Electromagnetism, gravity, the forces of movement and inertia. Internal alchemy of emotional release, opening chakras, awakening kundalini etc.

Procedure:

1. Fire Temple opening
2. Sixth Enochian Key
3. Seventeenth Enochian Key
4. Vibrate: Three Names of God (OIP TEAA PDOCE), Elemental King (EDLPRNAA), Six-lettered Name to conjure (VADALI), Five-lettered Name to control (OBAUA), Servient Angel's name

Kakodaimons
Water of fire

IGM, INM	- Water dominance
TEC, TOP	- Fire dominance
OAM, OOX	- Earth influence
MBR, MAP	- Air influence

(other permutations are also possible)

Purposes: Obtaining coined metal (Concealing Metals and Stones?)

Procedure:

1. Fire Temple opening
2. Sixth Enochian Key
3. Seventeenth Enochian Key
4. Vibrate: Three Names of God (OIP TEAA PDOCE), Elemental King (EDLPRNAA), Six-lettered Name to conjure (ILADAV), Five-lettered Name to control (AUABO), Kakodaimon's name.

Kerubic Archangel Earth of Fire

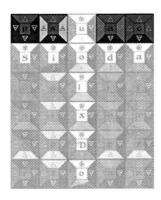

BPSAC

Purposes: Leading Kerubic Angels

Procedure:

1. Fire Temple opening
2. Sixth Enochian Key
3. Eighteenth Enochian Key
4. Vibrate: Three Names of God (OIP TEAA PDOCE), Elemental King (EDLPRNAA), Archangel's name (BPSAC)

Kerubic Angels
Earth of Fire

PSAC	-	Earth dominance
SACP	-	Air influence
ACPS	-	Water influence
CPSA	-	Fire dominance

Purposes: The knowledge of mechanical crafts, hand-crafts and arts. Precipitation, crystallization, and coming together of forms generally. Productive behaviors.

Procedure:

1. Fire Temple opening
2. Sixth Enochian Key
3. Eighteenth Enochian Key
4. Vibrate: Three Names of God (OIP TEAA PDOCE), Elemental King (EDLPRNAA), Archangel's name (BPSAC), Kerubic Angel's name

138

Servient Angels
Earth of Fire

DATT -   Fire dominance
DIOM -   Water influence
OOPZ -   Air influence
RGAN -   Earth dominance

(other permutations are also possible)

Purpose: Transformation. Processes of digestion, decomposition, solidification. Self Reinvention and personal transformation

Procedure:

1. Fire Temple opening
2. Sixth Enochian Key
3. Eighteenth Enochian Key
4. Vibrate: Three Names of God (OIP TEAA PDOCE), Elemental King (EDLPRNAA), Six-lettered Name to conjure (UOLXDO), Five-lettered Name to control (SIODA), Servient Angel's name

Kakodaimons
Earth of Fire

IDA, ITT	- Fire dominance
TDI, TOM	- Water influence
OOO, OPZ	- Air influence
MRG, MAN	- Earth dominance

(other permutations are also possible)

Purposes: (Destruction? Dissolution?)

Procedure:

1. Fire Temple opening
2. Sixth Enochian Key
3. Eighteenth Enochian Key
4. Vibrate: Three Names of God (OIP TEAA PDOCE), Elemental King (EDLPRNAA), Six-lettered Name to conjure (ODXLOU), Five-lettered Name to control (ADOIS), Kakodaimon's name

Kerubic Archangel
Fire of Fire

BZIZA

Purposes: Leading Kerubic Angels

Procedure:

1. Fire Temple opening
2. Sixth Enochian Key
3. Vibrate: Three Names of God (OIP TEAA PDOCE), Elemental King (EDLPRNAA), Archangel's name (BZIZA)

Kerubic Angels
Fire of Fire

ZIZA	-	Earth influence
IZAZ	-	Air influence
ZAZI	-	Water influence
AZIZ	-	Fire dominance

Purposes: The Secrets of Humanity. Energy and force. Values, passions, drives

Procedure

1. Fire Temple opening
2. Sixth Enochian Key
3. Vibrate: Three Names of God (OIP TEAA PDOCE), Elemental King (EDLPRNAA), Archangel's name (BZIZA), Kerubic Angel's name

142

Servient Angels
Fire of Fire

ADRE -	Fire dominance
SISP -	Water influence
PALI -	Air influence
ACAR -	Earth influence

(other permutations are also possible)

Purpose: The Knowledge of the creatures of the four elements. Life processes- sex, eating, death etc. Using the powers of the four elements to reorient and change inner drives and passions

Procedure:

1. Fire Temple opening
2. Sixth Enochian Key
3. Vibrate: Three Names of God (OIP TEAA PDOCE), Elemental King (EDLPRNAA), Six-lettered Name to conjure (RZIONR), Five-lettered Name to control (NRZFM), Servient Angel's name

Kakodaimons
Fire of Fire

IAD, IRE	- Fire dominance
TSI, TSP	- Water influence
OPA, OLI	- Air influence
MAC, MAR	- Earth influence

(other permutations are also possible)

Purposes: (Negative or destructive use of the four elements?)

Procedure:

1. Fire Temple opening
2. Sixth Enochian Key
3. Vibrate: Three Names of God (OIP TEAA PDOCE), Elemental King (EDLPRNAA), Six-lettered Name to conjure (RNOIZR), Five-lettered Name to control (MFZRN), Kakodaimon's name

Chapter Seven
Basic Ritual Technologies

There are ten basic steps to any magical invocation (or evocation) ritual, although some older forms of ritual omit "banishing rituals." Nonetheless these have become very embedded into modern magical culture, so we can safely consider them a part of the general formulae.

1. Decide upon the being with which you will communicate.
2. Banish you work area.
3. Purify your work area.
4. Consecrate your work area.
5. Oath/Statement of intent.
6. Preliminary Invocation of Higher Consciousness
7. Invoke the being.
8. Communicate with the being.
9. License to depart.
10. Banish your work Area.

You will see this structure in almost any magical ritual, and even find it within the more "magical" tools of the New Hermetics. To this basic outline we will also add elemental temple openings for work with the watchtowers, and planetary openings for work with the Heptarchia. But these ten steps should be included in every ritual. You may also wish to ritually bathe and don ceremonial robes previous to these steps.

There are also several pieces of ritual technology that will assist you to get the most out of your efforts. The following ritual techniques will be useful in all three parts of this magical work,

work with the watchtower angels, work with the thirty aethyrs and work with the Mystical Heptarchy. These techniques may seem familiar to some of you, but contain refinements suitable for the adept of the New Hermetics. It must be added that these are my techniques, and you should not feel enslaved to them in any way. They should be adjusted, through your own unique experiences in working with them, into paths to power for yourself. That being said, in my experience these techniques create true mystical experiences within ritual that can expand your consciousness and power to new heights. When you are conducting these techniques correctly, you will experience numerous ecstasies throughout your ritual work.

Erecting the Temple

In your ceremonies you will want to, as much as possible, make your physical working space conterminous with your inner temple. This will allow all of your previous work to come into play in your conjurations. The following will help to achieve this effect.

1. Sit in the middle of your circle and enter the altered state.

2. Enter your inner temple.

3. Move your conception of your inner temple in whatever way is necessary to place it exteriorly around you more completely in physical space. For some, your temple may already somewhat coincide with your physical space, but for others this may involve enlarging it, shrinking it, lowering it, or else just expanding it outward into your room.

4. Use breathing and charging spaces techniques to charge each wall of the temple/quadrant of the circle with the appropriate elemental energy. If possible, this should be done strongly enough to "see" with eyes open.

Do not be concerned if your physical workspace is of a completely different shape or size than your inner temple. The important issue is that you are connecting the two places in your consciousness.

Purification and Consecration

These are covered well in *The Book of Magick Power*, and can be augmented with the advanced adept techniques if you are familiar with these. This is easier to do than it might appear at first glance.

1. When moving around your temple with water to purify, once you have filled yourself with purifying light, feel the purifying light from above rushing down through your arms into the water, transforming the water into purifying nectar.

2. As you sprinkle it, visualize that the drops of water are pure light essence that is expanding to completely purify your space. This is actually easier done than said.

3. With consecration, expand your inner fire into the smoke of the incense in the same way.

Invoking Cosmic Consciousness

The angel Ave said, "Invocation proceedeth of the good will of man, and of the heat and fervency of the spirit: And therefore is prayer of such effect with God." The Chaldean Oracles say, "Enflame thyself with praying." This is really the critical component to your success.

I define cosmic consciousness as a state in which you are experiencing omnipresence, love for all things, omniscience and omnipotence. While you may not experience all of these in their entirety as a consciously felt sense in every experiment, it is necessary to cultivate this kind of consciousness in order to place yourself in sympathy with angelic consciousness. This can be achieved in a general sense from leading a "pure and holy life," but it can also be achieved by expanding your awareness in any number of ways. Those suggested in *The New Hermetics* will work quite well, and the even more advanced practices such as "The Lion Serpent" or the practice called "The Body of Λογοσ και Σοφια" if you are familiar with them. The key is that you must be in a state where you "feel" it could be possible to commune with angels. This is an entirely subjective experience, but one that you will easily recognize when you experience it. The critical factors seem to be a sense of expansion in which you experience your sense of bodily consciousness as "loosened from its physical sheath," and experience of "warmth and pure love," an experience of a "deeper connection" with everything around you, and a sense of "heightened capabilities." As you can probably notice, this is merely a lesser form of the components of cosmic consciousness as described above.

Some may say that they have experienced communication with the Enochian angels in other states than the ones described above, but these guidelines will assist you to effectively and con-sistently enter into communion. The following simple steps are sufficient if you have been working with any form of magical awakening for any length of time.

1. Imagine a globe of light above your head, glowing brightly. This light is your connection to cosmic awareness, a portal to the divine realm.

2. Experience this light shining down into you, filling your head, shoulders, torso, arms, and whole body with radiant light.

3. Experience this palpably, as an ecstasy that is transforming you into a more divine state.

4. Fill your whole being with this light. Allow this experience to become as ecstatic as possible, creating as complete a connection with this divine light as possible.

5. Experience this as a complete transformation into a divine being.

Many other variations on this are of course possible.

Rending the Veil

This is a gesture from the Golden Dawn that is extremely useful for "opening" the watchtowers as well as the aethyrs and the heptarchic realms. This should not be done merely as a gesture, but considered a true piercing of the veils into the magical plane. It can be conducted physically or mentally but in either case you should endeavor to perceive a real opening, by imagining that you are grabbing hold of two halves of a curtain and pulling them apart to open a palpable connection with the unknown.

1. Place your open hands in front of you at shoulder level, palms outward, knuckles touching.

2. Push your hands slightly forward, imagining that you are taking hold of a pair of astral veils.

3. Pull your arms apart, separating these astral curtains. Experience the energy of the region that you are opening palpably washing over you.

At the end of your operations you will simply to do this in reverse to symbolize, and actualize, the "Closing of the Veil." It should be noted that if you are using a crystal or magick mirror, this gesture can also be used to open and close the visionary space you are creating in the device.

Vibration of Divine Names

This technique should be used with all the angelic names in invocation, as well as for every word of the Enochian Keys. In vibrating names the most common instruction is to draw the energy of the name down from the light above, continuing down the middle pillar into your feet and then to utter the word as if it is thundering to the far reaches of the universe.

This method can be improved. For most, while the feet are rooted to the earth, they are not the core. A superior method involves drawing the energy into the heart or the muladhara. This can be further expanded so that we are drawing in the energy to the very core of the earth itself. This can be further expanded so that we are drawing the energy into the core of the universe itself. Finally, this can be perfected by the realization that the heart, the muladhara, earth core and core of the universe are ultimately conterminous. In your magical universe, these are all one. When you draw all to a point within the muladhara, the perineum, the veritable center of all things, the word that comes forth from this place is the "Word of God" that creates all things, a "big bang" which begins the universe anew according to your will. This is a true vibration of a God Name. Those familiar with the "Lion Serpent" advanced adept exercise will recognize its basic equivalent in this in an active form. The following can be improved by a thorough working knowledge of that technique.

1. Concentrate on the globe of light above your head. Draw in a breath, experiencing the power of universal consciousness entering with the breath, and flowing down your central channel. You may think about the name you are about to pronounce or not. It is not of great importance. You may also imagine the energy associated with the name (Fire, Jupiter,

etc) as coming in as a color or feeling with your respiration through the side channels or your pores.

2. All should be brought down to a point in your perineum, with total concentration.

3. The next thought to enter your consciousness should be the word or name you are expressing, and this should rush forth from your lips with the expiration.

4. Send all of the energy from the perineum up the central channel and out of your mouth (through the throat chakra).

5. Experience the word or name reverberating through the universe, renewing and transforming all of creation with the power of your speech.

Success in this is unmistakable. Draw in light from cosmic consciousness for every VIBRATION including all of the keys, sending it out with the words in different ways in different cases...

- For the three mystical god names, as a powerful wave across the landscape of the quadrants, awakening them
- For Tablet of Union names another wave, more undulatory, breathing out life and power
- For Kings, a spiraling force, like the spiral of the name
- For Calling Angelic beings, a beckoning beam, seeking its target
- For the Enochian keys a radiant, vibratory outpouring, with the fervent burning love of a sincere prayer

In reading or reciting the Enochian keys, you can vary the technique slightly, allowing several words or phrases with each expiration.

When you are calling a specific angel or angels, I recommend using the following simple invocation after reciting the appropriate keys:

"Zacar(e) od Zamran ils gah (angel's name) Dooiap (hierarchical name) od (hierarchical name) [adding as many hierarchical names as necessary] Zacare od Zamran ils gah (angel's name)"

Which translates approximately to:

"Move therefore and show yourself oh thou spirit (angel's name) In the name of (hierarchical name) and (hierarchical name) [adding as many hierarchical names as necessary] Move therefore and show yourself oh thou spirit (angel's name)"

You can also simply vibrate the appropriate hierarchy of names after the key. I prefer the simple little invocation above, but it is ultimately up to you.

Tracing Pentagrams and Hexagrams

Ritual tracing and visualization of pentagrams and hexagrams is obviously not part of the original procedures of Dee's Enochian explorations. These were added into the system by the

Golden Dawn. But they are quite useful ritual procedures that create an "anchor" to the various invoked energies the more times that you use them, and I see them as quite a useful addition to the magical ritual arsenal. But, generally speaking, you can use the same energy that you used in vibrating God names to trace pentagrams or hexagrams for banishings and invocations. As you trace the lineal figures you should be concentrating and drawing with enough focus that you can perceive them with eyes open or closed. You should trace them slowly and well enough that a sensitive (i.e.: imaginative) person in the circle with you would be able to see them too. For this and many other reasons the figures should be large, as large as possible, three to five feet in height depending on your reach.

Keep in mind that in an uncluttered temple space it should be possible to proceed through your rituals with your eyes open during the whole opening procedures. But if you are forced to practice in an area in which there are extraneous objects or things on the walls, you can close your eyes at the critical ritual moments to keep your spiritual eye focused on the magick and avoid irrelevant distractions.

1. Concentrate on the globe of light above your head. Draw in a breath, experiencing the power of universal consciousness entering with the breath, and flowing down your central channel.

2. At the same time imagine the energy that you are invoking with the lineal figure you are about to trace (Fire, Jupiter, etc) as coming in as a color or feeling with your respiration. This energy can flow down the side channels, on either side of the central channel or through your pores, if you can imagine this.

3. All should be brought down to a point in your perineum, with total concentration.

4. As you exhale, send the whole of this energy up the central channel and through your arm into the implement you are using to trace the figure (wand, cup, dagger etc.). Trace the figure in one long slow exhale.

5. See the energy pulsing around the lineal figure, creating your magical intention. The lineal figure is a representation of your will expressed symbolically and energetically, invoking the energy that you are contacting. You can experience this figure as drawing the appropriate energy from all around you into a coherent force, like a magnet drawing iron filings out of a pile of dust.

Circumambulation

When invoking energies, you may wish to walk around the edge of your circle, guiding the invoked energy into your space. The easiest manner of doing so is as follows.

1. Go to the edge of your circle from which you are drawing in the energy. Conduct whatever ritual actions you wish to invoke the energy.

2. Turn clockwise and throw your arms out to shoulder level before you, sending the energy into the circle.

3. Walk around the edge of your circle, guiding the energy in.

4. As you again reach the spot where you invoked the energy, repeat the gesture of projecting the energy into the circle.

5. You can continue in this as many times as you wish. For planetary energies, you may wish to circumambulate the circle the number of times associated with the planet. (three for Saturn, four for Jupiter, five for Mars etc.)

Visionary Techniques

The most important thing to understand in seeing angelic visions is that you must develop patience. There are several basic techniques that you can use in getting to the right place for receiving visions, but you must be patient even with these techniques. Do not expect the vision to commence instantly. Allow it to develop as naturally as possible. Dee and Kelly would sometimes wait for an hour or more before a vision opened up.

Of course you will be working within a more strictly magical context than they were, and your visions will most likely occur more swiftly. But be patient with yourself. The following techniques may be useful in discovering the best way for you to open up your visionary talents. You can experiment with any or all of them to help decide what is best for your personal needs.

Simple Reception

With this technique you will complete the keys and vibration of the hierarchies of names of the angels and then simply place your attention on the appropriate quadrant and experience the being you have invoked in whatever way it appears. Just open your inner eye and look into the gateway. The angel will appear in some way, and then you can converse. Use your own wisdom and test the spirits as you can. It may be that you need to vibrate the names several times before the true communication can begin.

Crystal Gazing

This technique is the one used by Edward Kelly in the original reception of this system. Gazing into crystals or magick mirrors used to be one of the most popular methods of spirit communication. It only fell out of favor in the twentieth century, and I think this is a shame. I think the reason it has fallen out of favor has to do with two factors. First and foremost I think it is related to the "psychologizing" of magick that has taken place in the last sixty years. If these "beings" are just "in our minds" then there is little difference between seeing them in a crystal and just seeing them with our eyes closed. But these angels are much more than just fantasies, and looking at them in the crystal can help you to grasp this more effectively. This does not mean that seeing them with eyes closed is less effective or real. It is just that the crystal helps you to see that they are in fact "other" intelligences somewhat more clearly. The second reason that this technique has fallen out of favor is that it is a bit more difficult than just closing one's eyes and allowing some sort of vision to develop. In using a skrying device you must allow the visionary state to develop with open eyes, and this is not easy for every-one. But it is this same state that allows abilities like seeing auras or clairvoyance in general.

The basic technique is essentially identical to the last except that you will look into a crystal ball, dark mirror or some other skrying device to develop the vision. You can even use the "image streaming" technique outlined below, or any of the others while looking into the skrying device.

I am not trying to force you to use a skrying device. If you have a preferred method, by all means use it. But I want you to be aware of this technique, and aware that it is valid and viable.

Telesmatic Imaging

Telesmatic imaging is covered more extensively in *The Book of Magick Power* than I have space for here. It is an active technique for developing a vision in which the occult attributions of the letters of a being's name are used to develop an image of the being based on the attributions. These are personifications of the energies of astrological symbols, colors, tarot images etc. This artificial image is maintained until it becomes animated and housed by the spirit. This technique can also be combined with the above techniques. The attributions of the Enochian alphabet generally used by the Golden Dawn are somewhat different from Hebrew. They are:

A		Taurus
B		Aries
C, K		Fire
D		Spirit
E		Virgo
F		Cauda Draconis
G		Cancer
H		Air
I, J, Y		Sagittarius
L		Cancer
M		Aquarius
N		Scorpio
O		Libra
P		Leo
Q		Water
R		Pisces
S		Gemini
T		Caput Draconis
U, V, W		Capricorn
X		Earth
Z		Leo

Rising on the Planes

In this variation you will send your consciousness out into the gateways of the watchtowers or the aethyrs and rise up and up until you come to a scene or a being. This is a variation on the New Hermetics technique, based on Crowley's "Liber O." You will need to test each vision for accuracy. It may take more than one "rising" to reach the true angel.

Gateways

You can also consciously create a gateway similar to the ones you have created for entering Tarot Cards. In this you can either use an image of the watchtower or the appropriate subquadrant of the watchtower, or you could use the "pyramid" created by Golden Dawn technique of turning the letter squares into pyramids. The appropriate pyramid to use would be the one related to the first letter of the angel's name. Again, you will need to test each vision for accuracy. You could also use the names or seals of the heptarchic princes, or the name of the appropriate aethyr in this.

Image Streaming

This is a highly optional technique, but one that I have found quite useful for the past several months in my practical explorations. It can be usefully combined with any of the above techniques. Many years ago I noticed something curious in my ritual magick work, which at that time was quite conservative and traditionally focused along the Golden Dawn via Aleister Crowley and Israel Regardie vein. What I noticed was that my visionary experiences were quite different in times when I was working with a group or a "magus and skryer" combination in comparison with times when I was working on my own. I found myself experiencing much more vivid and compelling visions when working with others. When I practiced on my own I found my experiences with ceremonial invocation, and particularly evocation, to be far less effective than those occasions of group work. My ability to communicate with the entity was severely limited, and the effectiveness of "results" oriented work was weakened. This is not to say that I never got results on my own, they were merely limited. At the time I chocked it up to the "gestalt" of group work, and the "tradition" that working with the "magus and skryer" combination was somehow just essentially "better." I eventually created several tools that helped me to accomplish this sort of work on my own, but I still felt that working with others opened up a different sort of experience. A perfect example of this sort of effect occurred during one of my New Hermetics classes. One of the adepts said that he had been having trouble with the "Tarot Trump Pathworking," so we did one with him right in the class. It was no surprise to me that he found himself much more capable in class than he had been on his own. He was experiencing the "gestalt" of the group.

But I wasn't entirely satisfied with the idea that the seer requires a magus and vice versa. For me, extensive use of body of light and the pathworking techniques had helped significantly in the effectiveness of my own work. I felt that there must be something else going on than merely the power of "group."

Then, one fine morning I started thinking about a book I'd had in my library for years by a gentleman named Wim Wenger, called "The Einstein Factor." It outlines a very simple technique called "Image Streaming" for entering into your own inner visionary stream to improve your intelligence and creativity by connecting with your "right brain." The technique was so simple that I'd virtually ignored it. But that day something occurred to me- the key to this technique is to *speak aloud* while visualizing, and to either speak aloud to *another person,* or to speak aloud *into a recording device* . According to Wenger, the speaking *must* be received by another party, whether a physical person or an audio recorder. It suddenly dawned on me that this might be the real answer to the mystery. After experimenting for the last few months I can say with a fair degree of certainty that this is the answer to the gestalt of the group. It is not the magick of working with others that improves the visionary state, but rather the magick of speaking aloud to "someone" while in the visionary state that produces more powerful results.

The key seems to be the ability to enter into a profoundly altered awareness while maintaining a conscious presence in that state. Speaking aloud *continuously throughout* your entrance into the visionary state seems to create just such an ability. I have found this technique so effective that I have experimentally added it into my New Hermetics supervision program. The principles of this technique are extremely simple.

The three critical factors of this exercise:

- You must describe your experiences **out loud**, preferably to an audio recorder or another person.

- You must describe everything that you experience in as many different sensory modalities as possible.

- You must describe everything in the present tense.

These three factors create a feedback loop that will strengthen your connection with your inner experience in a surprisingly powerful way. By speaking aloud you are keeping yourself alert, as well as encouraging your consciousness to produce more experiences. By using a recording device, you are emphasizing to your consciousness that what you are doing is important enough to preserve. By describing things with multiple senses you are enriching and enlivening your current experience, and by describing things in the present tense you are maintaining your conscious presence with the image and further enriching your connection.

When you are entering into the vision, just begin by noticing what you see behind your closed eyes (or in a scrying stone), whether it is a fuzzy greyness, dots of light or pictures forming. Describe your experience to yourself consciously **out loud**. This will spark your subconscious to throw up more and more images. In this I am talking about LITERALLY ANY image that pops into your mind, however faint or fleeting. Even if it just wavy squiggles or pure darkness, describe it to yourself out loud with as many sensory modalities as you can. Even if the image disappears you can keep describing it and adding more details.

At this stage it is perfectly okay and even helpful to just MAKE UP more sensory experiences than you are actually having. This is a variationon telesmatic imaging, and will encourage more of these types of experiences to occur.

If you have properly conducted your ceremony, everything that comes to mind will relate to the operation. I have found that the angels are fairly quick to appear. As more things pop into your mind continue to describe them to yourself **out loud**, connecting with them through your other senses as well, how the fleeting images you see might feel or sound or taste or smell. Just let your imagination flow. Images may only last a moment or two. Call them back by imagining interacting with them with your other senses. If you aren't sure about your other senses you can make things up. Pretend that you are smelling and tasting things. Describe these experiences **out loud**. As images become more and more tangible begin holding onto them, allowing scenes to develop, continuing to describe these scenes **out loud**. in as many different sensory terms as possible.

Practicing this just a few times will make you quite adept. Applying this technique to ritual invocation is incredibly easy. Simply have a recording device (or a human assistant, although in this day and age a recording device is far more reliable) in your circle and turn it on when you reach the point in your ritual that you are going to begin your communion with a spiritual being. Use you meditation anchor and take a few deep breaths, then direct your attention to the place where you have been manifesting the being. Describe the rest of your experience aloud. This may sound mind-bogglingly simple and almost inane, but you will be quite surprised at how effective this simple concept can be at freeing up your visionary muscles.

Personally, in my recent work I have often used this technique along with the "Music Only" New Hermetics CD[3]. I do this for several reasons. The sound of the music is a strong anchor for my altered state, it has imbedded binaural beats that

---

[3] This CD is given to students who enroll in the New Hermetics Supervision and Certification course.

encourage low alpha and theta brainwaves, that is brainwaves associated with trance states, and the headphones act as buffer for extraneous household noise. But you do not need to follow me in this unless you wish to. Also, mind machines could be used for this purpose. But nothing so elaborate is necessary.

Your Visions

It may take you more than one experiment to make real contact, and it may take many experiments for you establish effective communication in either direction. You would not expect to sit down at a piano for the first time and be able to play as well as Mozart. Neither should you expect your initial workings to resemble those of Edward Kelly or Aleister Crowley. But you will eventually succeed in discovering your own best ways to conduct this work, and you will be amazed by the transformations it creates in your life.

You may initially find your experiences coming through one or more sensory modalities more than others. You may see things and be unable to hear them. You may hear voices with no images. You may just "feel" that there is another presence with you. While these experiences can be valid and useful, do not allow yourself to let this be the pinnacle of your effort. Cultivate all five of your inner planes senses so that you can experience this communication as fully as possible. Believe me, it can be done. I was certainly not always as adept as I am today.

But you need to start somewhere. The practices outlined in the next chapter will enable you to get started connecting with this system, and should form your first practical work in this process. By the time you are done with the following exercises, you will be well on your way to being a true Enochian magician.

Chapter Eight
Getting Started: The Preliminary Workings

The work in this chapter is based upon the actual brief instructions given to Dee by the Angels. These angels gave Dee some simple and clear preliminary work to conduct before actively working with these angels. This instruction has all but been ignored by most modern magicians seeking access to this system. For many reasons, I think this preliminary work is highly important, and I hope that you will engage it before any other work in this book, even if you have done experiments in Enochian magick before.

The first instruction was to create a book containing the names of the angels and their conjurations. This was to be a grimoire of this magical system. Dee seems to have done this, and the manuscript resides at the British Library, Sloane #3191. This book that you're holding in your hands right now can be considered this sort of grimoire. You could also copy out all of the pertinent information into your own special book. But I see this as optional since this book contains both the names of the angels and their conjurations.

The second instruction was as follows:

> *"Four dayes... must you onely call upon those names of God [the twelve mystical names] ... And 14 dayes after you shall... call the Angels by Petition, and by the name of God, unto the which they are obedient. The*

15th day you shall Cloath your selves, in vestures made of linnen, white: and so have the apparition, use, and practice of the Creatures. For, it is not a labour of years, nor many dayes."

Before beginning your active operations you would be wise to conduct this simple eighteen-day preliminary operation to fully open and connect with the watchtowers. This eighteen-day operation is prescribed as above in Dee's diaries but it is also, from a pragmatic perspective, an excellent opportunity to get used to the operations and ritual procedures. By the time you are done with the eighteen days, you will be very comfortable with these ritual procedures, and your connection with the Enochian system will be undeniable. This brief extended operation can be seen as a sort of "magical retirement" in which you are focusing your consciousness as much as possible on connecting with this magical world. It is not necessary to take time off from work, or to seclude yourself from your family, but if you have this available to you it might add more power to this operation.

For the first four days, conduct the following ritual at least once a day, preferably twice or even thrice if you have the time. The specific wording of this ritual and all other rituals can of course be changed to suit your personal predilections. I instruct you to use the New Hermetics Grounding and Centering Ritual throughout, but you may certainly use the Lesser Banishing Ritual of the Pentagram or any other opening ritual you prefer instead.

Active Spirit · Passive Spirit

Invoking Spirit Pentagrams

Active Spirit · Passive Spirit

Banishing Spirit Pentagrams

Air · Water

Earth · Fire

Invoking Elemental Pentagrams

Air · Water

Earth · Fire

Banishing Pentagrams

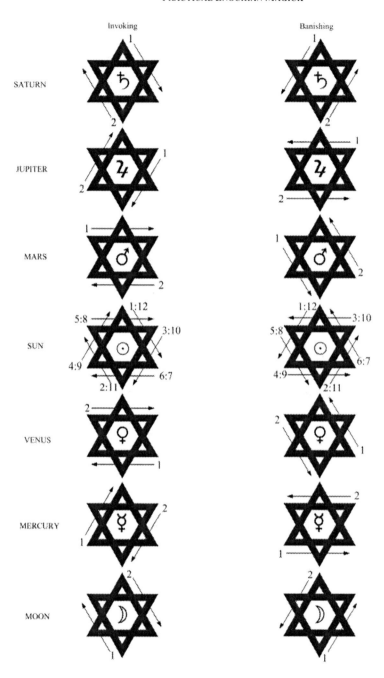

Hexagrams of the Planets

First Ritual for Activating
The Four Watchtowers

(to be conducted at least once a day, for four consecutive days)

Your temple should be set up as in the New Hermetics Self-Initiation Ritual, or with the Four Elemental Weapons on the altar. The tablets may be on the altar or the walls as well.

Sit in your temple and enter the altered state. Use your powers of visualization to make your Inner Temple conterminous with the room or temple in which you are physically sitting, (or else merely visualize that you are in both places at once).

Begin by Generating Rosicrucian Love.[1]

Perform the New Hermetics Grounding & Centering ritual.

Purify and consecrate your workspace.

Knock once on top of your altar.

Visualize the light above your head as shining down into you and filling you completely with the divine energy of cosmic consciousness. Numerous techniques for drawing down cosmic consciousness can be used. Those described in The New Hermetics are perfectly sufficient, although the advanced techniques of "The Lion Serpent" and/or "The Body of Λογοσ και Σοφια" could also be used. In any case this should bring on a powerful ecstasy, in which you say:

"I call upon the divine power of cosmic consciousness to bring real strength into my words and actions, by the twelve secret names of the most high, *(vibrate)* ORO, IBAH, AOZPI, OIP,

---

[1] See *The New Hermetics Equinox Journal Volume 1* for instruction in this practice, Dedicating Merit, the New Hermetics Grounding and Centering ritual and other advanced practices.

TEAA, PDOCE, MPH, ARSL, GAIOL, MOR, DIAL, HCTGA, I powerfully conjure the divine majesty within and without so that all of the angelic spirits of the four watchtowers may be called from their respective parts of the universe, through the special power of these holy names. Let them come quickly to me, visibly and peacefully, in friendship. Let them come and go by my will, giving reverence and obedience to these twelve mystical names. I command that they happily satisfy me in all things and at all times in my life, by accomplishing what I ask, if not by one means then by whatever means is best, goodly and perfectly in absolute completeness, according to each of their virtues and powers. *(vibrate)* AUM AUM AUM."

Knock once.

Go to the Eastern edge of your circle.

Make the sign of Rending the Veil, saying:

"In the Three great Secret Names of God, ORO IBAH AOZPI that are borne upon the Banners of the East, I open and activate my communication with the spirits of the watchtower of the east."

Take up the Rose or Dagger.

Make the Invoking Pentagram of Spirit Active with weapon, vibrating:

"EXARP"

Make the Invoking Pentagram of Air, vibrating:

"BATAIVAH"

Go to the Southern edge of your circle.

Make the sign of Rending the Veil, saying:

"In the Three great Secret Names of God, *(vibrate)* OIP TEAA PDOCE that are borne upon the Banners of the South, I open and activate my communication with the spirits of the watchtower of the South."

Take up the candle or wand.

Make the Invoking Pentagram of Spirit Active, vibrating:

"BITOM"

Make the Invoking Pentagram of Fire, vibrating:

"EDLPERNA"

Go to the Western edge of your circle.

Make the sign of Rending the Veil, saying:

"In the Three great Secret Names of God, *(vibrate)* MPH ARSL GAIOL that are borne upon the Banners of the West, I open and activate my communication with the spirits of the watchtower of the west."

Take up the Cup.

Make the Invoking Pentagram of Spirit passive, vibrating:

"HCOMA"

Make the Invoking Pentagram of Water, vibrating:

"RAAGIOSL"

Go to the Northern edge of your circle.

Make the sign of Rending the Veil, saying:

"In the Three great Secret Names of God, *(vibrate)* MOR DIAL HCTGA that are borne upon the Banners of the north, I open and activate my communication with the spirits of the watchtower of the north."

Take up the Disk or Pantacle.

Make the Invoking Pentagram of Spirit Passive, vibrating:

"NANTA"

Make the Invoking Pentagram of Earth, vibrating:

"ICZHIHAL"

Sit and recite the first key (Ol Sonf Vorsg…)

Close with the New Hermetics Grounding & Centering ritual.

Dedicate the Merit.

After conducting the ritual above for four days, conduct the following expanded ritual for the following fourteen days.

Second Ritual for Activating the Four Watchtowers and the Heptarchia

(To be conducted at least once a day, though preferably two to three times a day, for fourteen days following the first four)

Your temple should be set up as in the New Hermetics Self-Initiation Ritual, or with the Four Elemental Weapons on the altar. The tablets may be on the altar or the walls as well.

Sit in your temple and enter the altered state. Use your powers of visualization to make your Inner Temple conterminous with the room or temple in which you are physically sitting, (or else merely visualize that you are in both places at once).

Begin by Generating Rosicrucian Love

Perform the New Hermetics Grounding & Centering ritual.

Purify and consecrate your workspace.

Knock once on top of your altar.

Visualize the light above your head as shining down into you and filling you completely with the divine energy of cosmic consciousness. Numerous techniques for drawing down cosmic consciousness can be used. Those described in The New Hermetics are perfectly sufficient, although the advanced techniques of "The Lion Serpent" and/or "The Body of Λογοσ και Σοφια" could also be used. In any case, This should bring on a powerful ecstasy, in which you say:

"I call upon the divine power of cosmic consciousness to bring real strength into my words and actions, by the twelve secret names of the most high, *(vibrate)* ORO, IBAH, AOZPI, OIP, TEAA, PDOCE, MPH, ARSL, GAIOL, MOR, DIAL, HCTGA, I powerfully conjure the divine majesty within and without so that all of the angelic spirits of the four watchtowers may be called from their respective parts of the universe, through the special power of these holy names. Let them come quickly to me, visibly and peacefully, in friendship. Let them come and go by my will, giving reverence and obedience to these twelve mystical names. I command that they happily satisfy me in all things and at all times in my life, by accomplishing what I ask, if not by one means then by whatever means is best, goodly and perfectly in absolute completeness, according to each of their virtues and powers. *(vibrate)* AUM AUM AUM."

Vibrate the first key. (Ol Sonf Vorsg…)

Knock once.

Go to the Eastern edge of your circle.

Make the sign of Rending the Veil, saying:

"In the Three great Secret Names of God, ORO IBAH AOZPI that are borne upon the Banners of the East, I open and activate my communication with the spirits of the watchtower of the east."

Take up the Rose or Dagger.

Make the Invoking Pentagram of Spirit Active with weapon, vibrating:

"EXARP"

Make the Invoking Pentagram of Air, vibrating:

"BATAIVAH"

Vibrate the third key (Micma goho…) *then say:*

"By these further names *(vibrating all these names as appropriate)* HABIORO, AAOZAIF, AHAOZPI, AVTOTAR, HTMORDA, HIPOTGA, the six seniors, as well as these most sacred names ERZLA, EYTPA, ETNBR, EXGSD, and these IDOIGO, ARDZA, LLACZA, PALAM, AIAOAI, OIIIT, AOVRRZ, ALOAI, I most powerfully invoke and conjure the angels of the watchtower of the east."

Go to the Southern edge of your circle.

Make the sign of Rending the Veil, saying:

"In the Three great Secret Names of God, *(vibrate)* OIP TEAA PDOCE that are borne upon the Banners of the South, I open and activate my communication with the spirits of the watchtower of the South."

Take up the candle or wand.

Make the Invoking Pentagram of Spirit Active, vibrating:

"BITOM"

Make the Invoking Pentagram of Fire, vibrating:

"EDLPERNA"

Vibrate the sixth key (Gah S Diu…) then say:

"By these further names *(vibrating all these names as appropriate)* ALNDVOD, AAPDOCE, ARINNAP, AAETPIO, ADOEOET, ANODOIN, the six seniors, as well as these most sacred names BDOPA, BANAA, BPSAC, BZIZA, and these NOALMR, OLOAG, VADALI, OBAUA, UOLXDO, SIODA, RZIONR, NRZFM, I most powerfully invoke and conjure the angels of the watchtower of the South."

Go to the Western edge of your circle.

Make the sign of Rending the Veil, saying:

"In the Three great Secret Names of God, *(vibrate)* MPH ARSL GAIOL that are borne upon the Banners of the West, I open and activate my communication with the spirits of the watchtower of the west."

Take up the Cup.

Make the Invoking Pentagram of Spirit passive, vibrating:

"HCOMA"

Make the Invoking Pentagram of Water, vibrating:

"RAAGIOSL"

Vibrate the fourth key (Othil Lasdi...) *then say:*

"By these further names *(vibrating all these names as appropriate)* LAOAXRP SONIZNT LSRAHPM SLGAIOL LIGDISA SAIINOV the six seniors, as well as these most sacred names HTAAD, HTDIM, HMAGL, HNLRX, and these OBGOTA, AABCO, NELAPR, OMEBB, MALADI, OLAAD, IAAASD, ATAPA, I most powerfully invoke and conjure the angels of the watchtower of the West.

Go to the Northern edge of your circle.

Make the sign of Rending the Veil, saying:

"In the Three great Secret Names of God, *(vibrate)* MOR DIAL HCTGA that are borne upon the Banners of the north, I open and activate my communication with the spirits of the watchtower of the north."

Take up the Disk or Pantacle.

Make the Invoking Pentagram of Spirit Passive, vibrating:

"NANTA"

Make the Invoking Pentagram of Earth, vibrating:

"ICZHIHAL"

Vibrate the fifth key (Sapa Zimii...) then say:

"By these further names *(vibrating all these names as appropriate)* LAIDROM, ALHCTGA, AHMLICV, ACZINOR, LIIANSA, LZINOPO, the six seniors, as well as these most sacred names NBOZA, NPHRA, NOCNC, NASMT, and these ANGPOI, VNNAX, ANAEEM, SONDN, ABALPT, ARBIZ, OPMNIR, ILPIZ, I most powerfully invoke and conjure the angels of the watchtower of the North."

Knock once upon the altar.

[Here you may now invoke the appropriate angels from the Heptarchia, using the following formula for each day. In other words, on Monday, you will invoke the Prince and King of Monday and so on for each day].

Trace first triangle of the appropriate planetary Invoking Hexagram, Vibrate the appropriate name of the Son of light (see Part Three of this book)

Trace second triangle Vibrate the appropriate name of the Son of Son of Light (see Part Three of this book) then say:

"By the noble prince *(vibrate name)* and the puissant king *(vibrate name)* I most powerfully invoke and conjure the angels of *(day)*.

Knock once upon the altar.

Sit or stand in your circle, Vibrate second key (Adgt vpaah...)

Close with the New Hermetics Grounding & Centering ritual.

Dedicate the Merit.

Practical Work

Once you have conducted the above operation you will be ready to really begin your practical work. I suggest that you begin this process by reviewing your goals, or even conducting the New Hermetics goal-setting workshop.[1] Doing this will allow you to really connect with how you can apply this magick in a practical way.

Discover in yourself what areas could use an influx of the energies and knowledge of these beings. For each goal, ask yourself the following sorts of questions which will help you to choose appropriate beings for communion:

- What element does this goal correspond to most closely? Is there a secondary element in the goal? Is there a third?

- How would I categorize the goal elementally and sub-elementally? (i.e. A fiery goal with a bit of a watery undertone, an air goal that contains water and earth issues as well, etc.)

- What is presently standing in the way of me accomplishing this goal? What resources do I need to accomplish this goal?

- Is there some new knowledge that I need in order to obtain this goal? New beliefs? Are there hidden blocks?

---

[1] The Initiate Level workbook that contains this workshop can be downloaded from www.newhermetics.com.

Chapter Nine
Elemental Temple Openings

The following ritual procedures can be conducted for working with each of the tablets. Again, please feel free to adjust any wording that does not suit your needs. These rituals are merely meant to be suggestive of the process to be undertaken. I do not expect you to feel compelled to work with them exactly as written. This procedure combined with the specific outlines in Chapter Six will allow you to proceed with almost any conceivable operation within the watchtowers.

Opening of the Temple for Workings with the Air Tablet

Your temple should be set up as above.

Sit in your temple and enter the altered state. Use your powers of visualization to make your Inner Temple conterminous with the room or temple in which you are physically sitting, (or else merely visualize that you are in both places at once).

Begin by Generating Rosicrucian Love.

Perform the New Hermetics Grounding & Centering ritual.

Purify and consecrate your workspace.

Knock once on top of your altar.

Invoke Cosmic Consciousness, stating the purpose of your ritual.

Knock once.

Go to the Eastern edge of your circle. Face the East, visualizing the yellow air wall vividly before you, saying:

"By the force of KNOWLEDGE creatures of Air, powers of the East, be with me. Move for me as the breath that moves upon the face of the earth, and the breath that moves in and out of my body. Open my mind and let the clouds of thought clear. Be prompt and active. Even as I breathe, as the breath of life flows through me, spirits of air awaken through the power of INTELLIGENCE."

Make the sign of Rending the Veil, saying:

"In the Three great Secret Names of God, ORO IBAH AOZPI that are borne upon the Banners of the East, I open and activate my communication with the spirits of the watchtower of the east."

Take up the Rose or Dagger.

Make the Invoking Pentagram of Spirit Active with weapon, vibrating:

"EXARP"

Make the Invoking Pentagram of Air, vibrating:

"BATAIVAH"

Say, "The Spirits of Air are invoked!"

Knock: 333 --- 333 --- 333

Vibrate the third key (Micma goho…) and any other keys as necessary for subquadrants, then invoke the specific angel using the appropriate hierarchical names.

Opening of the Temple
for Workings with the Water Tablet

Your temple should be set up as above.

Sit in your temple and enter the altered state. Use your powers of visualization to make your Inner Temple conterminous with the room or temple in which you are physically sitting, (or else merely visualize that you are in both places at once).

Begin by Generating Rosicrucian Love.

Perform the New Hermetics Grounding & Centering ritual.

Purify and consecrate your workspace.

Knock once on top of your altar.

Invoke Cosmic Consciousness, stating the purpose of your ritual.

Knock once.

Go to the Western edge of your circle. Face the West, visualizing the blue water wall vividly before you, saying:

"By the force of DARING Creatures of Water, powers of the West, be with me. Flow for me like the mighty oceans deep, and the watery blood that pulsates through my body. Awaken my heart to love and bliss, and agony of ecstasy. Be flexible and attentive. Even as the water of my body moves in rhythmic

179

motion through the dance of life, spirits of water awaken through the power of UNDERSTANDING."

Make the sign of Rending the Veil, saying:

"In the Three great Secret Names of God, *(vibrate)* MPH ARSL GAIOL that are borne upon the Banners of the West, I open and activate my communication with the spirits of the watchtower of the west."

Take up the Cup.

Make the Invoking Pentagram of Spirit passive, vibrating:

"HCOMA"

Make the Invoking Pentagram of Water, vibrating:

"RAAGIOSL"

Say, "The Spirits of Water are invoked."

Knock: 1 --- 333 --- 1 --- 333.

Vibrate the fourth key (Othil Lasdi…) *and any other keys as necessary for subquadrants, then invoke the specific angel using the appropriate hierarchical names.*

Opening of the Temple for Workings with the Earth Tablet

Your temple should be set up as above.

Sit in your temple and enter the altered state. Use your powers of visualization to make your Inner Temple conterminous with the room

or temple in which you are physically sitting, (or else merely visualize that you are in both places at once).

Begin by Generating Rosicrucian Love.

Perform the New Hermetics Grounding & Centering ritual.

Purify and consecrate your workspace.

Knock once on top of your altar.

Invoke Cosmic Consciousness, stating the purpose of your ritual.

Knock once.

Go to the Northern edge of your circle. Face the North, visualizing the black earth wall vividly before you, saying:

"By the force of SILENCE Creatures of Earth, powers of the North, be with me. You support and shape me through the bones and sinews of my body, whose rigidity sustains me. Awaken my body, to move and to be still. Be laborious and patient. Even as our skin and bones contain and maintain us, spirits of earth awaken through the power of MANIFESTATION."

Make the sign of Rending the Veil, saying:

"In the Three great Secret Names of God, *(vibrate)* MOR DIAL HCTGA that are borne upon the Banners of the north, I open and activate my communication with the spirits of the watchtower of the north."

Take up the Disk or Pantacle.

Make the Invoking Pentagram of Spirit Passive, vibrating:

"NANTA"

Make the Invoking Pentagram of Earth, vibrating:

"ICZHIHAL"

Say, "The Spirits of Earth are invoked!"

Knock: 4444 --- 333 --- 22 --- 1.

Vibrate the fifth key (Sapa Zimii…) and any other keys as necessary for subquadrants, then invoke the specific angel using the appropriate hierarchical names.

Opening of the Temple for Workings with the Fire Tablet

Your temple should be set up as above.

Sit in your temple and enter the altered state. Use your powers of visualization to make your Inner Temple conterminous with the room or temple in which you are physically sitting, (or else merely visualize that you are in both places at once).

Begin by Generating Rosicrucian Love.

Perform the New Hermetics Grounding & Centering ritual.

Purify and consecrate your workspace.

Knock once on top of your altar.

Invoke Cosmic Consciousness, stating the purpose of your ritual.

Knock once.

Go to the Southern edge of your circle. Face the South, visualizing the red fire wall vividly before you, saying:

By the force of WILL, Creatures of Fire, powers of the South, be with me. Burn for me as the life force driving me forward, whose life is the life of every star, and every cell in my body. Awaken my power, the force and will to live and love. Be energetic and strong. Even as the heat of my body rises in the fervor of this rite, spirits of fire awaken through the power of CREATION.

Make the sign of Rending the Veil, saying:

"In the Three great Secret Names of God, *(vibrate)* OIP TEAA PDOCE that are borne upon the Banners of the South, I open and activate my communication with the spirits of the watchtower of the South."

Take up the candle or wand.

Make the Invoking Pentagram of Spirit Active, vibrating:

"BITOM"

Make the Invoking Pentagram of Fire, vibrating:

"EDLPERNA"

Say, "The Spirits of Fire are invoked!"

Knock: 333 --- 1 --- 333.

Vibrate the sixth key (Gah S Diu…) and any other keys as necessary for subquadrants, then invoke the specific angel using the appropriate hierarchical names.

frequency of Practice

So, we have now gone over the essential components to a simple approach to working with the Enochian watchtowers. I wish you great adventures in this inner journey. The question of how often one should conduct these sorts of practices often comes up, and a wide variety of answers are given out by authorities of many stripes. My advice to you is that you conduct your spiritual exercises as often as you feel moved to do so. My own practice goes through very active phases, usually when I am searching out new knowledge, to quite dormant periods where I do no Enochian magick for several months at a time. When I am active, I usually work daily.

Dee and Kelly seemed to have had a similar rhythm, as did Aleister Crowley. The correct frequency of your practice is the one that assists you in your growth as an adept. I will leave you with this quote from Aleister Crowley. "You have got to go out Rising on the Planes every day of your life, year after year. You are not to be disheartened by failure, or too much encouraged by success, in any one practice or set of practices. What you are doing is what will be of real value to you in the end; and that is, developing a character, creating a Karma, which will give you the power to do your will."[1]

---

[1] Crowley, Aleister. *Magick: Liber ABA* p. 249

Part Two

The Magick of the Thirty Aethyrs

Chapter Ten
The Aethyrs

Approaching visionary work with the thirty aethyrs or the ninety-one "governors" is theoretically much more straightforward than anything else in the Enochian system. There is only one key for all thirty aethyrs, the only difference being the name of the aethyr recited toward the beginning of each key. The aethyrs received little attention in the original official Golden Dawn instruction, but constituted the majority of Aleister Crowley's own personal magical work with the Enochian system.

There are many ambiguities with these aethyrs. While there is a diagram in Dee's notes like the one on the following page, and clearly the aethyrs were meant to be considered concentric planes in Dee's conception, Dee's work with the aethyrs and their "governors" seems much more concerned with different regions of the Earth, rather than spiritual dimensions. It seems that while these governors had their abode in ever-higher spiritual planes, their function was practical control over various regions of the Earth. Aleister Crowley also noticed this discrepency[1] and chose basically to ignore it and explore the thirty aethyrs, in a long series of visions, as expansive planes of spiritual development in and of themselves. It is unclear how familiar he was with Dee's firsthand work.

The whole concept of exploring the aethyrs as spiritual planes was really invented by Crowley or one of his Golden Dawn mentors. But some of Crowley's most profound magical

---

[1] Crowley, Aleister. *The Vision and the Voice* p. 8

and spiritual experiences transpired in his visions within these aethyrs, and this work is certainly worthy of attention.

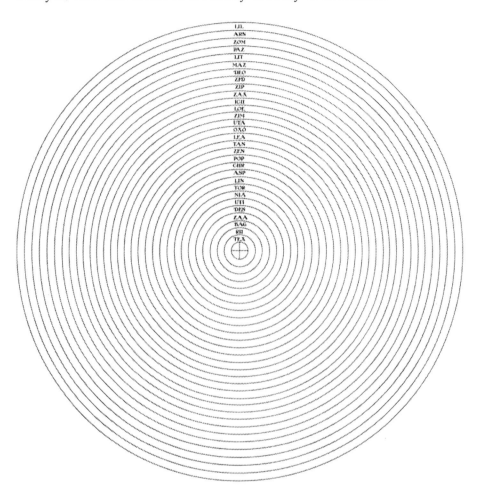

DIAGRAM 14 - THE THIRTY AETHYRS

Notably, within his vision of the 18th aethyr, Crowley received an instruction in how to approach visions of the aethyrs[1] He did not use this instruction in his further work, and it is unclear whether it is really necessary. He never seemed to separate it out as an instruction in its own right, or even mentioned it much elsewhere in his writings. We will adopt a

---

[1] ibid. pp. 115-116

few ideas from that instruction, and you can read it in that work and consider the rest for yourself.

But what are these aethyrs exactly? We can see them quite easily as expansive spiritual planes, but it is only natural to ask, "What is the nature of each of these planes?" The challenge that presents itself to us in trying to understand the progressive structure of these aethyrs is that they do not neatly fit into any of our current popular models of the higher worlds.

Several modern authors, including Crowley, have attempted to offer roadmaps of these aethyrs. Crowley's model is based entirely on his own practical experience of each of these aethyrs. He started with a more or less Qabalistic approach, but the aethyric experiences led him to a very unique classification. It is highly idiosyncratic, and far too complex for me to present it effectively in these pages.

Pat Zalewski suggests a simple and elegant model[1] in which the aethyrs are spread throughout the upper three of the four sub-worlds of the world of Assiah in the Qabala, Atziluth of Assiah, Briah of Assiah, and Yetzirah of Assiah, one aethyr for each sephirah in each of these sub-worlds. In his scheme, the governors then occupy the fourth and lowest world, Assiah of Assiah, spread throughout each sephirah in clusters. However, the problem with this model is that it simply does not at all fit the specific communications of the angels, who stated clearly that the governors dwell in the aethyrs themselves. Nonetheless it is a workable model in and of itself.

Gerald Schueler proposes another model to explain the nature of the aethyrs by placing them into the Eastern Gupta-Vidya model.[2] Of course the aethyrs do not fit into this model perfectly either. Schueler then goes on to describe in great detail what an explorer will experience in each aethyr. To me this is taking things a bit far. Individual experiences are so variable that such a cut and dry explanation seems to take the mystery out of the process.

---

[1] Zalewski, Pat *Golden Dawn Enochian Magic,* p. 41
[2] Schueler, Gerald *Enochian Magic* p. 238

It is also popular among many modern writers to compare these aethyrs with the Aeons of certain gnostic systems. If that was what Dee or Kelly had imbedded in their unconscious from studying the writings of the early church fathers, then the system of Valentinus the gnostic seems the most likely candidate as it contained thirty aeons and was discussed at length repeatedly by the Polemicists. So, here is a side by side comparison of the Thirty Aeons as they were described by Ireneaus, Tertullian and Epiphanius along with the thirty aethyrs.

Aethyr	Aeon	Greek of Aeon
LIL	Depth (or Pre-beginning)	Bythos (Proarche)
ARN	Silence (or Thought)	Sige (Ennoia)
ZOM	Mind (or One-begotten)	Nous (Monogenes)
PAZ	Truth	Aletheia
LIT	Word	Logos
MAZ	Life	Zoe
DEO	Man	Anthropos
ZID	Church	Ecclesia
ZIP	Profound	Bythius
ZAX	Mixture	Mixis
ICH	Never old	Ageratos
LOE	Union	Henosis
ZIM	Essential nature	Autophyes
VTA	Pleasure	Hedone
OXO	Immoveable	Acinetos
LEA	Commixture	Syncrasis
TAN	Only-begotten	Monogenes
ZEN	Happiness	Macaria
POP	Comforter	Paracletus
CHR	Faith	Pistis
ASP	Paternal	Patricos
LIN	Hope	Elpis
TOR	Maternal	Matricos
NIA	Love	Agape
VTI	Praise	Ainos

DES	Intelligence	Synesis
ZAA	Son of Ecclesia	Ecclesiasticus
BAG	Blessedness	Macariotes
RII	Perfect	Theletos
TEX	Wisdom	Sophia

So much for the thirty aeons and the thirty aethyrs. If you would like to carry this comparison out further you may discover something worthwhile. I have not. But what all of these models have in common is only that as one travels up through the aethyrs one is moving into more and more rarified spiritual states. This seems to be the only unifying theme within the various viewpoints, and to me seems the only definition that is really necessary.

If you are visiting the thirtieth or twenty-ninth aethyrs of TEX and RII you are going to be visiting planes quite close to physical reality and your experiences will generally be those related to astral phenomena. But as you get closer and closer to the first aethyr LIL your experiences will be getting into entirely spiritual territory. You could divide the spaces up amongst any of various models for higher consciousness, but your own practical experiences should be considered the safest guide.

The adventure of exploring these aethyrs is often considered an advanced and required rite of passage, particularly amongst Thelemic adepts. It certainly formed an important stage in the magical work of Aleister Crowley. But this is only one pathway up the mountain of initiation, one of many available to adepts of all traditions.

This work is quite tranformative, at least if you allow it to be. I have not explored all thirty aethyrs, but those that I have explored have left me changed, in ways that are often only tangentially related to the visions I've received.

If you are going to explore this journey, I suggest working with the aethyrs slowly and progressively. Allow yourself several experiences of each aethyr before moving on if necessary. At least wait until you have had a significant experience within each aethyr. Each vision will be unique and offer new insights into the aethyr and your expansion. It may take several workings or several lifetimes to get through many of the aethyrs. There is no rush.

Don't expect your visions to coincide with those of Crowley or anyone else. Crowley was going through a stage in his own personal magical awakening as he conducted his visions of the aethyrs, and these visions took place at a distinct moment in time. Your journey is different, and your real visions will be too.

Some occultists make a pageant out of Crowley's visions, reenacting them as a sort of pathworking or even ritual theater. While this might be entertaining or amusing, it will most likely not result in much real progress. Allow your experiences to develop as they will. There is a unique magical adventure in each of these aethyrs that is waiting just for you.

Chapter Eleven
The Ninety-One Governors

Dee and Kelly received ninety-one names and sigils relating to ninety-one regions of the Earth, sometimes called "Governors." The sigils of these beings are actually found within the watchtowers. Every capitalized letter in the watchtowers begins the name of one of these governors, and tracing the path of the rest of the letters of the name creates the sigil. These governors are associated with the thirty aethyrs, but they are governors of earthly regions, in fact they are "God's" names for these regions, and the spirits associated with these names are the guiding genii of these various locales. These earthly regions are based on the areas described in *Agrippa's Three Books of Occult Philosophy*,[1] which in turn are based on Ptolemy's *Tetrabiblos*[2]. But many of these place names seem rather obscure to me and are not to be found in Ptolemy. (Dee felt the same way!)

At any rate, it seems doubtful that these governors bear much relation to the aethyrs when considered as concentric expanding spiritual planes. The names of these governors are clearly associated with places on the Earth, such as Ethiopia or India, as well as other unknown places. The exact purpose that these names served is not entirely clear, although it seems that they could depose corrupt leaders in those areas. Perhaps an operation of this sort might be in order in certain areas of the globe today!

Some magicians vibrate the names of one or all of these governors when conducting visionary working with the aethyrs, but

---

[1] Agrippa, Henry C. *Three Books of Occult Philosophy, Book 1 Ch. 31*, p. 97
[2] Ptolemy, Claudius. *Tetrabiblos, Loeb Classical Library, Volume 1*, p. 159

there is nothing regarding this matter in Dee's notebooks. But then there is nothing about visionary work with the aethyrs at all in Dee's work.

Crowley mentions very little about these governors in *The Vision and the Voice* except in passing, and it seems quite clear that in that work he was just reciting the keys and experiencing an ensuing vision. He did not invoke the governors in his workings. On a few occasions he conducted extensive formal rituals around his work in the aethyrs, but in none of it is there any mention of the governors. Although Crowley speaks to an angel in each aethyr, this angel is not one of the "governors." In fact the angels give Crowley names on occasion, which are consistently not the name of any governor, although one angel's name is constructed from the names of several of these governors together. Crowley's basic technique appears to be related to a Golden Dawn practice. In this practice the adept travelling in the spirit vision finds an "angelic guide" at the beginning of the vision to help him or her navigate the "countryside" of the plane being visited.

Nonetheless, many modern manuals on Enochian magick suggest that you contact these governors when working with the aethyrs. I have even done so myself. I've communicated with some of these "governors," and received useful instruction. I know of other magicians who have done the same thing. But I still don't see them as an essential part of the process when you are exploring the aethyrs.

However, you may be interested in exploring work with the governors in a way that more closely relates to the original work of Dee. In this case, the aethyrs in and of themselves do not play much of a role in the work at all. Instead you will be contacting the guiding genii of the different regions of the Earth.[1] To do so you will conduct a ritual working in which you use the call of the appropriate aethyr for the governor you wish to contact, and then call the governor with the name of one of twelve Angel

---

[1] These regions are often incomprehensible in Dee's lists. See *The New Hermetics Equinox Journal Volume 1* for an article on these regions.

Kings that rule over the governors. Further you will face one of twelve compass points to do so. The following chart shows these relationships:

	Governor	Angelic King	Earthly Region	Direction
1	OCCODON	ZARZILG	Aegyptus	East NE
2	PASCOMB	ZINGGEN	Syria	West SW
3	VALGARS	ALPUDUS	Mesopotamia	West NW
4	DOAGNIS	ZARNAAH	Cappadocia	North
5	PACASNA	ZIRACAH	Tuscia	South
6	DIALOIA	ZIRACAH	Asia Minor	South
7	SAMAPHA	ZARZILG	Hyrcaina	East NE
8	VIROOLI	ALPUDUS	Thracia	West NW
9	ANDISPI	LAVAVOTH	Gosmam	South SE
10	THOTANP	LAVAVOTH	Thebaidi	South SE
11	AXXIARG	LAVAVOTH	Parsadal	South SE
12	POTHNIR	ARFAOLG	India	North NW
13	LAZDIXI	OLPAGED	Bactriane	East
14	NOCAMAL	ALPUDUS	Cilicia	West NW
15	TIARPAX	ZINGGEN	Oxiana	West SW
16	SAXTOMP	GEBABAL	Numidia	East SE
17	VAUAAMP	ARFAOLG	Cyprus	North NW
18	ZIRZIRD	GEBABAL	Parthia	East SE
19	OPMACAS	ZARNAAH	Getulia	North
20	GENADOL	HONONOL	Arabia	West
21	ASPIAON	ZINGGEN	Phalagon	West SW
22	ZAMFRES	GEBABAL	Mantiana	East SE
23	TODNAON	OLPAGAD	Soxia	East
24	PRISTAC	ZARZILG	Gallia	East NE
25	ODDIORG	HONONOL	Assyria	West
26	CRALPIR	LAVAVOTH	Sogdiana	South SE
27	DOANZIN	ZARZILG	Lydia	East NE
28	LEXARPH	ZINGGEN	Caspis	West SW
29	COMANAN	ALPUDUS	Germania	West NW
30	TABITOM	ZARZILG	Trenam	East NE
31	MOLPAND	LAVAVOTH	Bithynia	South SE
32	VSNARDA	ZURCHOL	Gracia	South SW
33	PONODOL	HONONOL	Lacia	West
34	TAPAMAL	ZURCHOL	Onigap	South SW

35	GEDOONS	CADAAMP	India Major	North NE
36	AMBRIOL	ZIRACAH	Orchenij	ZIRACAH
37	GECAOND	LAVAVOTH	Achaia	South SE
38	LAPARIN	OLPAGED	Armenia	East
39	DOCEPAX	ALPUDUS	Nemrodiana	West NW
40	TEDOOND	GEBABAL	Paphlogonia	East SE
41	VIUIPOS	ALPUDUS	Phasiana	West NW
42	VOANAMB	ARFAOLG	Chaldei	North NW
43	TAHAMDO	ZARZILG	Itergi	East NE
44	NOTIABI	LAVAVOTH	Macedonia	South SE
45	TASTOZO	ARFAOLG	Garamannia	North NW
46	CUCNRPT	ZIRACAH	Sauromatica	South
47	LAVACON	HONONOL	Aethiopia	West
48	SOCHIAL	ARFAOLG	Fiacim	North NW
49	SIGMORF	ZIRACAH	Colchica	South
50	AYDROPT	OLPAGED	Cireniaca	East
51	TOCARZI	ZARZILG	Nasamoma	East NE
52	NABAOMI	GEBABAL	Carthago	East SE
53	ZAFASAI	ALPUDUS	Coxlant	West NW
54	YALPAMB	ARFAOLG	Adumea	North NW
55	TORZOXI	ARFAOLG	Parstavia	North NW
56	ABRIOND	CADAAMP	Celtica	North NE
57	OMAGRAP	ZINGGEN	Vinsan	West SW
58	ZILDRON	GEBABAL	Tolpam	East SE
59	PARZIBA	HONONOL	Carcedoma	West
60	TOTOCAN	ALPUDUS	Italia	West NW
61	CHIRZPA	ARFAOLG	Brytania	North NW
62	TOANTOM	CADAAMP	Phenices	North NE
63	VIXPALG	ZURCHOL	Comaginen	South SW
64	OSIDAIA	ARFAOLG	Apulia	North NW
65	PAOAOAN	OLPAGED	Marmarica	East
66	CALZIRG	ARFAOLG	Concava Syria	North NW
67	RONOOMB	ZARNAAH	Gebal	North
68	ONIZIMP	LAVAVOTH	Elam	South SE
69	ZAXANIN	ZINGGEN	Adunia	West SW
70	ORANCIR	ZARNAAH	Media	North
71	CHASLPO	LAVAVOTH	Arriana	South SE
72	SOAGEEL	ZINGGEN	Chaldea	West SW
73	MIRZIND	ZARNAAH	Serica Populi	North

74	OBUAORS	ZIRACAH	Persia	South
75	RANGLAM	ARFAOLG	Gongatha	North NW
76	POPHAND	ARFAOLG	Gorsin	North NW
77	NIGRANA	CADAAMP	Hispania	North NE
78	LAZHIIM	ARFAOLG	Pamphilia	North NW
79	SAZIAMI	ZIRACAH	Oacidi	South
80	MATHVLA	ZARNAAH	Babylon	North
81	CRPANIB	GEBABAL	Median	East SE
82	PABNIXP	LAVAVOTH	Adumian	South SE
83	POCISNI	ZARZILG	Foelix Arabia	East NE
84	OXLOPAR	ZURCHOL	Metagonitibim	South SW
85	VASTRIM	HONONOL	Assyria	West
86	ODRAXTI	ZARNAAH	Affrica	North
87	GMTZIAM	ARFAOLG	Bactriani	North NW
88	TAAOGBA	ARFAOLG	Asnan	North NW
89	GEMNIMB	ZARNAAH	Phrygia	North
90	ADVORPT	HONONOL	Creta	West
91	DOXMAEL	ZURCHOL	Mauritania	South SW

The Angelic Kings that are hierarchically above the governors are zodiacal in nature, and related to the 12 Hebrew tribes. Dee used Agrippa to decide upon which zodiacal sign to assign to each Angelic King based on the twelve Hebrew tribes. However, the adepts of the Golden Dawn used their own theories about astrrology to make a somewhat different assignment. The early Qabalistic text Sepher Yetzirah offers a third possibility. These are far from the only possibilities for ways to attribute the signs of the Zodiac to the Tribes of Israel, but these are the most likely familiar to the Western esotericist. I place them all here with the Angelic rulers of the governors:

Angelic King	Tribe	Golden Dawn[1]	Sepher Yetzirah	Agrippa
Hononol	Judah	Leo	Aries	Gemini
Alpudus	Issaachar	Cancer	Taurus	Libra
Zinggen	Zebulon	Capricorn	Gemini	Aquarius

[1] It should be noted that in Pat Zalewski's *Golden Dawn Enochian Magic* an odd permutation of the tribes shifts the attributions around.

Ziracah	Reuben	Aquarius	Cancer	Taurus
Zurchol	Simeon	Pisces	Leo	Virgo
Lavavoth	Gad	Aries	Virgo	Capricorn
Arfaolg	Ephraim	Taurus	Libra	Pisces
Zarnaah	Manasseh	Gemini	Scorpio	Cancer
Cadaamp	Benjamin	Sagittarius	Sagittarius	Scorpio
Olpaged	Dan	Scorpio	Capricorn	Aries
Gebabal	Asher	Libra	Aquarius	Leo
Zarzilg	Naftali	Virgo	Pisces	Sagittarius

While I am providing these other two methods of assigning the zodiac for reference, I am fairly certain that it is Agrippa's attributions that should be used. The following chart shows all three, within Dee's diagram of the Angelic Kings. The outer circle is Agrippa's attributions, the middle is Sepher Yetzirah, and the innermost is the Golden Dawn zodiacal associations for the Hebrew tribes.

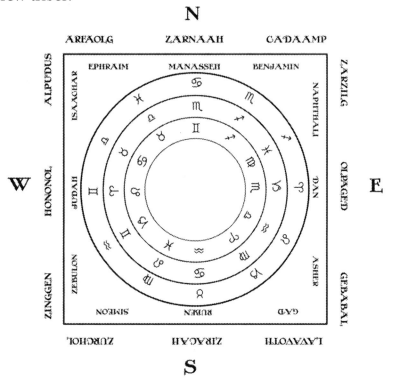

DIAGRAM 15 - THE DIRECTIONS OF THE ANGELIC KINGS

Only Agrippa's attributions create a meaningful pattern, and meaningful patterns are almost always present in Enochian Magick. Zodiacal rituals are easiest to perform as variations on planetary rituals using the hexagram of one of the seven planets that rules each sign. Although new relationships with the outer planets have been proposed for modern astrology, this innovation is unnecessary for your ritual magick, unless you feel compelled. The traditional rulerships of the planets are as follows:

Aries   Mars
Taurus   Venus
Gemini   Mercury
Cancer   Moon
Leo   Sun
Virgo   Mercury
Libra   Venus
Scorpio   Mars
Sagittarius Jupiter
Capricorn   Saturn
Aquarius   Saturn
Pisces   Jupiter

You can adapt the planetary openings in part three for this purpose quite easily. You could also try beginning the ceremony by opening the watchtower from which the name is drawn.

Even if you are mostly interested in the aethyrs as spiritual planes for exploration that doesn't mean you should necessarily ignore these governors. The governors can still be useful in understanding how to break through to higher levels or in evaluating a vision. If you wish to have a conversation with one of them, you may simply proceed as in watchtower invocations, but using the Key of the appropriate aethyr as the final key, or use a planetary/zodiacal opening. When you vibrate their name and the name of the angelic king above them in invocation, you should also trace the governor's sigil to lend power to the process. This can be done in the same way that you trace pentagrams and hexagrams. Here are the names of the Governors along with their aethyrs, tablets from which the names are drawn, and sigils below for your benefit.

Governor	Aethyr	Tablet	Sigil
1. OCCODON	LIL	WEST	
2. PASCOMB	LIL	WEST	
3. VALGARS	LIL	WEST	
4. DOAGNIS	ARN	WEST	
5. PACASNA	ARN	WEST	
6. DIALOIA	ARN	WEST	
7. SAMAPHA	ZOM	WEST	
8. VIROOLI	ZOM	WEST	
9. ANDISPI	ZOM	WEST	
10. THOTANP	PAZ	WEST	
11. AXXIARG	PAZ	WEST	
12. POTHNIR	PAZ	WEST	
13. LAZDIXI	LIT	WEST	
14. NOCAMAL	LIT	WEST	

15. TIARPAX	LIT	WEST	
16. SAXTOMP	MAZ	SOUTH	
17. VAUAAMP	MAZ	SOUTH	
18. ZIRZIRD	MAZ	SOUTH	
19. OPMACAS	DEO	SOUTH	
20. GENADOL	DEO	SOUTH	
21. ASPIAON	DEO	SOUTH	
22. ZAMFRES	ZID	SOUTH	
23. TODNAON	ZID	SOUTH	
24. PRISTAC	ZID	SOUTH	
25. ODDIORG	ZIP	SOUTH	
26. CRALPIR	ZIP	SOUTH	
27. DOANZIN	ZIP	SOUTH	
28. LEXARPH	ZAX	TABLET OF UNION	
29. COMANAN	ZAX	TABLET OF UNION	
30. TABITOM	ZAX	TABLET OF UNION	

31. MOLPAND	ICH	WEST
32. VSNARDA	ICH	WEST
33. PONODOL	ICH	SOUTH
34. TAPAMAL	LOE	SOUTH
35. GEDOONS	LOE	SOUTH
36. AMBRIOL	LOE	SOUTH
37. GECAOND	ZIM	SOUTH
38. LAPARIN	ZIM	SOUTH
39. DOCEPAX	ZIM	SOUTH
40. TEDOOND	VTA	SOUTH
41. VIUIPOS	VTA	SOUTH
42. VOANAMB	VTA	SOUTH
43. TAHAMDO	OXO	EAST
44. NOTIABI	OXO	EAST
45. TASTOZO	OXO	EAST
46. CUCNRPT	LEA	EAST

47. LAVACON	LEA	EAST
48. SOCHIAL	LEA	EAST
49. SIGMORF	TAN	EAST
50. AYDROPT	TAN	EAST
51. TOCARZI	TAN	EAST
52. NABAOMI	ZEN	EAST
53. ZAFASAI	ZEN	EAST
54. YALPAMB	ZEN	EAST
55. TORZOXI	POP	EAST
56. ABRIOND	POP	EAST
57. OMAGRAP	POP	EAST
58. ZILDRON	CHR	EAST
59. PARZIBA	CHR	EAST
60. TOTOCAN	CHR	EAST
61. CHIRZPA	ASP	EAST

62. TOANTOM	ASP	EAST
63. VIXPALG	ASP	EAST
64. OSIDAIA	LIN	EAST
65. PAOAOAN	LIN	ALL FOUR TABLETS
66. CALZIRG	LIN	NORTH
67. RONOOMB	TOR	NORTH
68. ONIZIMP	TOR	NORTH
69. ZAXANIN	TOR	NORTH
70. ORANCIR	NIA	NORTH
71. CHASLPO	NIA	NORTH
72. SOAGEEL	NIA	NORTH
73. MIRZIND	VTI	NORTH
74. OBUAORS	VTI	NORTH
75. RANGLAM	VTI	NORTH
76. POPHAND	DES	NORTH

77. NIGRANA	DES	NORTH
78. LAZHIIM	DES	NORTH
79. SAZIAMI	ZAA	NORTH
80. MATHVLA	ZAA	NORTH
81. CRPANIB	ZAA	NORTH
82. PABNIXP	BAG	NORTH
83. POCISNI	BAG	NORTH
84. OXLOPAR	BAG	NORTH
85. VASTRIM	RII	NORTH
86. ODRAXTI	RII	NORTH
87. GMTZIAM	RII	NORTH
88. TAAOGBA	TEX	WEST
89. GEMNIMB	TEX	WEST
90. ADVORPT	TEX	WEST
91. DOXMAEL	TEX	WEST

Chapter Twelve
Practical Working Procedures

As I mentioned above, in one of Aleister Crowley's visions of the aethyrs he received a detailed instruction in how to properly "partake of the mystery of the Aethyr."[1] But Crowley does not seem to have formalized this instruction into an official A∴ A∴ document as he did with his vision of the eighth aethyr.[2] Further, he did not use this instruction in any way for his continued work with the aethyrs. This always seemed curious to me, though I've never actually fully used this instruction in any experimental way in my personal work with the aethyrs.

However, there is one part of it that I've found very useful in my own work. He received a color for each of the aethyrs. In the instruction, this color is to be used as an ink in writing out the invocation. Generally I have adjusted this and used this color to formulate a vortex of energy, a swirling gateway into the aethyr.

30.	TEX	mixed colors
29.	RII	bluish-green
28.	BAG	indigo
27.	ZAA	angry clouds of ruddy brown
26.	DES	white flecked red, blue, yellow; edges green
25.	VTI	cold dark gray
24.	NIA	beetle-brown, blue-brown color

---

[1] This instruction is found in *The Vision and the Voice* 18th Aethyr pp. 115-116.
[2] Crowley received an instruction for attaining the "Knowledge and Conversation of the Holy Guardian Angel" in the 8th Aethyr, and subsequently published it separately as Liber VIII, an official "class D" instructional document for the A∴ A∴

23.	TOR	violet cobalt
22.	LIN	rose-madder
21.	ASP	pale green
20.	CHR	mauve
19.	POP	crimson adorned with silver
18	ZEN	bright yellow
17	TAN	crimson
16	LEA	pale blue
15.	OXO	olive
14	VTA	amber
13	ZIM	green-gray
12	LOE	russet
11	ICH	maroon
10	ZAX	black
9	ZIP	gray
8	ZID	indigo
7	DEO	orange
6	MAZ	sapphire
5	LIT	silver
4	PAZ	emerald
3	ZOM	violet
2	ARN	scarlet
1	LIL	gold

I have consistently found these colors to be extremely useful for opening gateways into each of the aethyrs I've explored.

As for the details of practically working with the aethyrs as spiritual planes for exploration, after many experiments, failures, half-successes and finally many enlightening experiences, my preferred method is as follows:

1. Enter the altered state through anchoring and deep breathing.

2. Make your inner temple conterminous with your physical workspace.

3. Generate Rosicrucian Love.

4. Perform the New Hermetics Grounding and Centering as a physical ritual.

5. Purify and consecrate circle.

6. Invoke Cosmic Consciousness, announcing what Aethyr you will visit.

7. Recite the Key of the Aethyr, visualizing the entry into the aethyr as a swirling gateway in the color suggested above, with the letters of the name of aethyr in flashing (or opposite) color glowing in the center of the aethric gateway. As you recite the key, drawing down energy from cosmic consciousness through your body with your in-breath, and as you speak send the energy into this gateway, to empower and strengthen the gate.

8. Sit down and re-anchor the altered state (probably just for good measure. You should be in a highly altered state!)

9. (At this point, after reciting the key myself, I put on headphones and turn on an audio recorder. I have created recordings of the Enochian keys by themselves along with the New Hermetics background music and binaural beats designed to ramp me into the theta brainwave state. This step is obviously optional!)

10. Allow your consciousness to rise up through the gateway, knowing that an experience of the aethyr is on the other side.

11. As you pass through the gateway a scene will eventually develop. Continue rising until it does so. Once you begin to see a scene, explore it. (I verbally describe my experience

aloud into my audio recorder). You may encounter beings, angels, vast hierarchies, strange alien landscapes and an infinite number of other possibilities.

12. When you feel that you have had enough, or you are ejected from the vision, return to your inner temple and your circle.

13. Banish the aethyr by imagining the gateway closing up and disappearing.

14. Perform the New Hermetics grounding and centering as a physical ritual.

This is just my technique. There are many variations that you could also try, just as in working with the Watchtower angels. You could simply rise up until a vision commences. You could just close your eyes and allow a vision to come as it will. You could also look into a crystal or black mirror.

If you are interested in invoking the governors you can proceed as in the watchtower ceremonies, but simply use the key of the appropriate aethyr and then invoke the governor(s) by the power of the angel that rules above them, tracing the governor's sigil in the air (or on the appropriate tablet) as you are invoking.

But it may be superior to open with one of the planetary openings from part three. Choose the planet that rules over the Angelic King that rules over the governor. Then if you trace the sigil from the appropriate tablet you will be combining all three parts of the Enochian system in a single ritual.

Part Three

The Magick of the Heptarchia Mystica

Chapter Thirteen
The Forty Nine Good Angels

To tell the truth, it was many years before I really even knew that this whole portion of Dee and Kelly's work existed. It is not discussed in most modern works that are wholly derived from the Golden Dawn system. When I discovered this system, these beings looked like just another set of planetary beings, which abound in medieval and renaissance magical literature. My first attitude was that it was just a prelude to the "real" magick of the watchtowers. But this system is actually quite unique when you understand it in greater detail. In many ways it is quite analogous to the four watchtowers, but containing planetary and sub-planetary angels. There is a Sun of Sun being, a Sun of Mercury being, a Sun of Venus being, and so on with the various permutations of planetary relationships. This fits very conveniently with the traditional system of magical planetary hours, and allows for a wide variety of practical explorations. There are also ministers for each day that operate for approximately 34 minute periods throughout each day. One aspect that makes this segment of Dee and Kelly's work so intriguing is that, unlike the watchtowers, we actually have records of their communication with many of these beings.

In my own experiments I have generally used techniques somewhat similar to the ones I gave in *The Book of Magick Power*, with a few notable modifications, and have met with promising results. The practical work as it follows in the next pages is largely my own unique interpretation of this system, but based on what I've pieced together from Dee. One interesting facet of this system is its use of multiple talismanic principles and I am currently exploring this more fully.

Reading Dee's diary entries relating to these heptarchical angels is a very strange experience. The spirits seem to be communicating a fairly ordered system, and yet it does not quite all add up. It is almost like waking up from a dream in which you feel like what you were dreaming about makes perfect sense, but then when you really think about it the whole experience was completely illogical.

This is not helped by the fact that several pages of Dee's journal related to the Heptarchia are missing. Nonetheless there are the rudiments of a system that is worthy of much more practical exploration. We will continue to take an eclectic approach to working with this system, combining elements of the original system with practical modern magick.

The Heptarchic system is somewhat reminiscent of the system set forth in the Arbatel of Magic, relating to the Olympic planetary spirits, or the Heptameron, allegedly written by Peter D'Abano. There are angels of the planets and the days of the week, and you can call them at those appropriate times. But the comparison is only superficial. The names and functions of the Angels are completely unique to this system, as was the way in which these names were received.

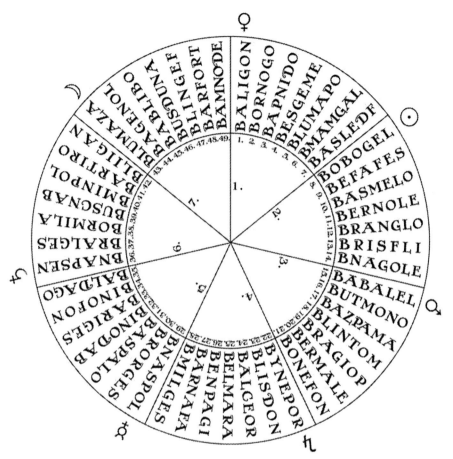

DIAGRAM 16- CIRCULAR CALENDAR OF THE GOOD ANGELS

215

Chapter Fourteen
The Seven Tables

This system of angels came to Dee and Kelly in a very circuitous manner. Initially, the names of these angels were received through a vision that revealed seven tables, each with seven by seven squares. The names of the angels are drawn from these squares, one letter from each tablet for the name of each angel. And these tablets in and of themselves are talismanic magical objects on their own, each having a specific practical purpose.

1 B	2 B	3 B	4 B	5 B	6 B	7 B
8 B	9 B	10 B	11 B	12 B	13 B	14 B
15 B	16 B	17 B	18 B	19 B	20 B	21 B
22 B	23 B	24 B	25 B	26 B	27 B	28 B
29 B	30 B	31 B	32 B	33 B	34 B	35 B
36 B	37 B	38 B	39 B	40 B	41 B	42 B
43 B	44 B	45 B	46 B	47 B	48 B	49 B

DIAGRAM 17- TABLE 1, FOR "WIT AND WISDOM"

7 A	21 O	1 A	26 E	45 A	24 A	13 R
34 I	5 O	29 N	2 O	33 A	6 M	25 E
49 A	4 E	35 A	40 M	18 L	25 M	23 L
39 V	47 L	3 A	5 L	15 A	36 N	30 R
20 E	19 R	43 A	37 R	32 I	17 A	41 A
10 A	38 O	16 V	27 A	12 R	43 R	22 Y
9 E	44 A	11 E	42 L	31 A	14 N	46 V

DIAGRAM 18- TABLE 2, FOR "THE EXALTATION AND GOVERNMENT OF PRINCES"

6 A	7 S	29 A	13 B	23 I	8 B	17 Z
36 A	39 S	12 A	30 O	1 L	10 S	21 N
5 V	31 S	25 L	43 B	26 N	32 N	3 P
18 I	19 A	48 R	4 S	27 R	34 N	24 L
38 R	44 G	37 A	20 R	16 T	2 R	22 N
49 M	43 U	35 R	47 I	9 F	33 R	42 I
15 I	46 S	11 R	41 R	40 I	25 I	14 A

DIAGRAM 19- TABLE 3, FOR "THE GAIN AND TRADE OF MERCHANDISE"

6 M	41 T	39 C	19 G	49 N	45 L	14 G
31 P	25 M	2 N	18 N	44 E	8 O	30 R
7 L	15 A	35 M	32 O	43 M	29 S	28 L
33 D	37 L	3 N	13 S	42 I	12 N	33 I
1 I	17 P	16 M	46 D	5 M	40 N	21 E
27 N	23 S	4 G	36 P	26 P	47 N	26 M
9 A	10 M	24 C	22 E	34 O	11 N	48 F

DIAGRAM 20- TABLE 4, FOR "THE GAIN AND TRADE OF MERCHANDISE"

G	I	O	O	Ā	Ā	O
D	I	N	F	G	I	I
E	Ā	O	Ā	G	E	T
Ā	G	Ā	Ā	P	L	P
G	D	P	G	G	Ā	V
G	F	E	E	F	G	F
S	I	Ā	O	N	O	G

DIAGRAM 21- TABLE 5, FOR "THE QUALITY OF EARTH, AND WATERS"

E	E	L	F	D	L	N
L	Ā	G	O	R	L	O
O	O	G	D	R	O	P
Ā	E	O	M	E	E	L
E	E	O	L	O	E	D
M	Ā	G	L	E	L	O
O	Z	R	O	B	Ā	Ā

DIAGRAM 22- TABLE 6, FOR "MOTION OF AIR AND THOSE THAT MOVE IN IT"

E	E	F	Ā	I	F	O
Ā	N	L	N	M	O	L
O	O	I	Ā	L	B	S
T	O	O	B	S	Ā	L
S	L	Ā	O	O	S	E
L	N	S	P	E	O	R
R	N	O	N	E	N	Ā

DIAGRAM 23- TABLE 7, FOR "WISDOM: FIRE"

There is a number, one through forty-nine, in each square along with each of the letters. Taking all of the squares that contain the number one in each of the tablets produces the name BALIGON. This process can be repeated forty-nine times, for each of the forty-nine numbers. Since the first tablet is entirely filled with "B," all of the angel names start with "B." This signifies that they are "bonorum" or "good." The angels that are drawn out are as follows:

No.	Name	Planet	Title	Day
1.	Baligon	Venus	King	Friday
2.	Bornogo	Venus	Prince	Sunday
3.	Bapnido	Venus	Governor	Tuesday
4.	Besgeme	Venus	Governor	Thursday
5.	Blumapo	Venus	Governor	Wednesday
6.	Bmamgal	Venus	Governor	Saturday
7.	Basledf	Venus	Governor	Monday
8.	Bobogel	Sol	King	Sunday
9.	Befafes	Sol	Prince	Tuesday
10.	Basmelo	Sol	Governor	Thursday
11.	Bernole	Sol	Governor	Wednesday
12.	Branglo	Sol	Governor	Saturday
13.	Brisfli	Sol	Governor	Monday
14.	Bnagole	Sol	Governor	Friday
15.	Babalel	Mars	King	Tuesday
16.	Butmono	Mars	Prince	Thursday
17.	Bazpama	Mars	Governor	Wednesday
18.	Blintom	Mars	Governor	Saturday
19.	Bragiop	Mars	Governor	Monday
20.	Bermale	Mars	Governor	Friday
21.	Bonefon	Mars	Governor	Sunday
22.	Bynepor	Jupiter	King	Thursday
23.	Blisdon	Jupiter	Prince	Wednesday
24.	Balceor	Jupiter	Governor	Saturday
25.	Belmara	Jupiter	Governor	Monday

26.	Benpagi	Jupiter	Governor	Friday
27.	Barnafa	Jupiter	Governor	Sunday
28.	Bmilges	Jupiter	Governor	Tuesday
29.	Bnaspol	Mercury	King	Wednesday
30.	Brorges	Mercury	Prince	Saturday
31.	Baspalo	Mercury	Governor	Monday
32.	Binodab	Mercury	Governor	Friday
33.	Bariges	Mercury	Governor	Sunday
34.	Binofon	Mercury	Governor	Tuesday
35.	Baldago	Mercury	Governor	Thursday
36.	Bnapsen	Saturn	King	Saturday
37.	Bralges	Saturn	Prince	Monday
38.	Bormila	Saturn	Governor	Friday
39.	Buscnab	Saturn	Governor	Sunday
40.	Bminpol	Saturn	Governor	Tuesday
41.	Bartiro	Saturn	Governor	Thursday
42.	Bliigan	Saturn	Governor	Wednesday
43.	Blumaza	Luna	King	Monday
44.	Bagenol	Luna	Prince	Friday
45.	Bablibo	Luna	Governor	Sunday
46.	Busduna	Luna	Governor	Tuesday
47.	Blingef	Luna	Governor	Thursday
48.	Barfort	Luna	Governor	Wednesday
49.	Bamnode	Luna	Governor	Saturday

Dee and Kelly communicated directly with almost all of the Kings and Princes listed above, but none of the governors beneath them. They received a highly unusual set of powers attributed to each of the kings and princes that we will discuss more fully in the next chapter.

Chapter Fifteen
The Heptarchic Hierarchy

The Heptarchy as a whole is ruled by an angelic being called King Carmara. Underneath him is Prince Hagonel, who does not seem to be the same Hagonel that also occurs as one of the other beings. They all seem to sprout from one root. and there seems to be a relationship of identity between these and several of the Kings and Princes. Ruling over each day of the week under Prince Hagonel are the Sons of Light and the Sons of the Sons of Light. These "sons" are all beings whose names occur on the Sigillum Dei Aemeth.

There is a King and a Prince for each day of the week (and hence each planet) and an additional five ministers. There are also an additional forty-two ministers for each half hour or so period throughout the day, on each day of the week. You can call forth any of these angels with the methods that follow. The names of the forty-two ministers for each day are based on some rather complex permutations of the names of the Kings. Instead of trying to give an explanation of this I will simply list them.

The purposes of these beings as they were given to Dee and Kelly do not really correspond much to the traditional planetary attributions. Pat Zalewski has suggested[1] that these purposes are more closely akin to the first seven days of creation in the Bible than the planets in any usual sense. But this comparison, although very clever, is only somewhat tangentially applicable. The chart on the following page shows some of the traditional correspondences of the planets, along with those given to Dee and Kelly by the Angels themselves.

---

[1] Zalewski, Pat *Golden Dawn Enochian Magic* p. 108

Planet	Qualities	Kings	Princes
Saturn:	Structures, limitation, responsibility, seriousness, reincarnation, death, inheritances, old age	King Bnapsen: casting out the power of wicked spirits	Prince Brorges: *(Mercury)* Active agent of his King
Jupiter:	Generosity, abundance, leadership, vision, acquiring wealth, legal issues, luck, expansion	King Bynepor: the general state and condition of all things	Prince Butmono: *(Mars)* life and breath in living Creatures
Mars:	Justice, strength, force, violence, energy, war, aggression, courage, competition, athletics, masculinity	King Babalel: Rules as King of the waters whose power is in the bowels of the waters	Prince Befafes: *(Sun)* The Seas, various aspects, and battles
Sun:	Harmony, balance, wholeness, health, regain youth, peace, illumination, obtaining money, divine power	King Bobogel: bestowing wisdom and knowledge	Prince Bornogo: *(Venus)* perfecting corrupted nature, the knowledge of metals
Venus:	Love, desire, aesthetics, nurture, beauty, pleasure, art, luxury, aphrodisiac, perfume, femininity	King Baligon: All that can be wrought in aerial Actions, (as Carmara, the teacher, orderer and disposer of the entire heptarcical doctrine)[1]	Prince Bagenol: *(Moon)* (as Hagonel, The whole operation of the Earth, commands the kings, princes and nobles of nature)[2]
Mercury:	Reason, communication, logic, knowledge, travel, writing, school, science, commerce, medicine, mathematics, the mind	King Bnaspol: the earth and bowels of the Earth	Prince Blisdon: *(Jupiter)* the keys of the mysteries of the Earth
Moon:	Imagination, instinct, subconscious, emotion, the astral world, clairvoyance, dreams, sleep, the sea	King Blumaza: discovering the divine mysteries, knowledge past, present and future[3]	Prince Bralges *(Saturn)* oversees the aerial invisible creatures living in his dominion.

---

[1] From Tyson, Donald *Enochian Magic for Beginners,* p. 136-7
[2] ibid.
[3] This purpose for King Blumaza is from *Golden Dawn Enochian Magic.* I do not find it in Dee's Journals, though it could be present somewhere. Dee mentions something about being in charge of Earthly kings, but this is not presented clearly.

This chart is curious, because Dee was a noted astrologer, and was very well aware of the traditional correspondences of the planetary powers. While in the renaissance these powers were perhaps a bit different from even the ones I listed above, they were close enough that the powers given by the kings and princes must have seemed quite odd. And yet Dee was not at all perplexed.

As you are working with these beings in practical magical operations, I would keep in mind these purposes delivered to Dee and Kelly, but you may also want to explore the more traditional planetary correspondences as well, and see how these beings react. My temple openings reflect this, by offering a more or less traditionally inspired planetary opening, and then calling the specific angels using what was delivered to Dee. But my limited personal experience has led me to believe that the functions of these angels as delivered to Dee were in response to his particular needs and interests at the time, and not the full breadth of their abilities and domain. This holds true for the angels of the watchtowers as well. For instance, the King and Prince of Tuesday (associated with Mars and Sun of Mars respectively) both stated that their powers were in the waters, and even related to battles in the waters. Well, England was heavily involved in maritime activities at this time, and the Spanish Armada was a threat. Dee also had a particular interest in naval matters, and wrote a book about creating the equivalent of the U.S. Coast Guard for England. It is easy to see why a Martial being could express an interest in the sea for Dee. Qabalistic exploration of the planetary correspondences to the sephiroth can give further ideas.

Planetary Hours

In traditional Medieval and Renaissance magick, one planet rules each day as a whole, and each hour of the day and the night individually. The following chart depicts these relationships, with the Heptarchic Angels corresponding.

Hours from Midnight to Midnight	Sun. The Sun	Mon. The Moon	Tues. Mars	Wed. Mercury	Thurs. Jupiter	Fri. Venus	Sat. Saturn
1	Mercury BARIGES	Jupiter BELMARA	Venus BAPNIDO	Saturn BLIIGAN	Sun BASMELO	Moon BAGENOL	Mars BLINTOM
2	Moon BABLIBO	Mars BRAGIOP	Mercury BINOFON	Jupiter BLISDON	Venus BESGEME	Saturn BORMIFA	Sun BRANGLO
3	Saturn BUSCNAB	Sun BRISFLI	Moon BUSDUNA	Mars BAZPAMA	Mercury BALDAGO	Jupiter BENPAGI	Venus BMAMGAL
4	Jupiter BARNAFA	Venus BASLEDF	Saturn BMINPOL	Sun BERNOLE	Moon BLINGEF	Mars BERMALE	Mercury BRORGES
5	Mars BONEFON	Mercury BASPALO	Jupiter BMILGES	Venus BLUMAPO	Saturn BARTIRO	Sun BAGNOLE	Moon BAMNODE
6	Sun BOBOGEL	Moon BLUMAZA	Mars BABALEL	Mercury BNASPOL	Jupiter BYNEPOR	Venus BALIGON	Saturn BNAPSEN
7	Venus BORNOGO	Saturn BRALGES	Sun BEFAFES	Moon BARFORT	Mars BUTMONO	Mercury BINODAB	Jupiter BALCEOR
8	Mercury BARIGES	Jupiter BELMARA	Venus BAPNIDO	Saturn BLIIGAN	Sun BASMELO	Moon BAGENOL	Mars BLINTOM
9	Moon BABLIBO	Mars BRAGIOP	Mercury BINOFON	Jupiter BLISDON	Venus BESGEME	Saturn BORMIFA	Sun BRANGLO
10	Saturn BUSCNAB	Sun BRISFLI	Moon BUSDUNA	Mars BAZPAMA	Mercury BALDAGO	Jupiter BENPAGI	Venus BMAMGAL
11	Jupiter BARNAFA	Venus BASLEDF	Saturn BMINPOL	Sun BERNOLE	Moon BLINGEF	Mars BERMALE	Mercury BRORGES
12	Mars BONEFON	Mercury BASPALO	Jupiter BMILGES	Venus BLUMAPO	Saturn BARTIRO	Sun BAGNOLE	Moon BAMNODE
1	Sun BOBOGEL	Moon BLUMAZA	Mars BABALEL	Mercury BNASPOL	Jupiter BYNEPOR	Venus BALIGON	Saturn BNAPSEN
2	Venus BORNOGO	Saturn BRALGES	Sun BEFAFES	Moon BARFORT	Mars BUTMONO	Mercury BINODAB	Jupiter BALCEOR
3	Mercury BARIGES	Jupiter BELMARA	Venus BAPNIDO	Saturn BLIIGAN	Sun BASMELO	Moon BAGENOL	Mars BLINTOM
4	Moon BABLIBO	Mars BRAGIOP	Mercury BINOFON	Jupiter BLISDON	Venus BESGEME	Saturn BORMIFA	Sun BRANGLO
5	Saturn BUSCNAB	Sun BRISFLI	Moon BUSDUNA	Mars BAZPAMA	Mercury BALDAGO	Jupiter BENPAGI	Venus BMAMGAL
6	Jupiter BARNAFA	Venus BASLEDF	Saturn BMINPOL	Sun BERNOLE	Moon BLINGEF	Mars BERMALE	Mercury BRORGES
7	Mars BONEFON	Mercury BASPALO	Jupiter BMILGES	Venus BLUMAPO	Saturn BARTIRO	Sun BAGNOLE	Moon BAMNODE
8	Sun BOBOGEL	Moon BLUMAZA	Mars BABALEL	Mercury BNASPOL	Jupiter BYNEPOR	Venus BALIGON	Saturn BNAPSEN
9	Venus BORNOGO	Saturn BRALGES	Sun BEFAFES	Moon BARFORT	Mars BUTMONO	Mercury BINODAB	Jupiter BALCEOR
10	Mercury BARIGES	Jupiter BELMARA	Venus BAPNIDO	Saturn BLIIGAN	Sun BASMELO	Moon BAGENOL	Mars BLINTOM
11	Moon BABLIBO	Mars BRAGIOP	Mercury BINOFON	Jupiter BLISDON	Venus BESGEME	Saturn BORMIFA	Sun BRANGLO
12	Saturn BUSCNAB	Sun BRISFLI	Moon BUSDUNA	Mars BAZPAMA	Mercury BALDAGO	Jupiter BENPAGI	Venus BMAMGAL

Most magicians advocate that these planetary hours should be calculated in a somewhat complicated way in which the periods from sunrise to sunset are divided by twelve, and the periods from sunset to sunrise are divided by twelve, resulting in different hour lengths throughout the year as the days and nights grow shorter and longer.[1] This instruction comes down to us in Agrippa and Liber Juratus, among other places. In the Heptameron we find this instruction, "But this is to be observed by the way, that the first hour of the day, of every Country, and in every season whatsoever, is to be assigned to the Sun-rising, when he first appeareth arising in the horizon: and the first hour of the night is to be the thirteenth hour, from the first hour of the day. But of these things it is sufficiently spoken." This instruction, while making it necessary to begin the first hour at sunrise, does not seem to require complex hourly computations. If you were to use the above chart in that way, you would shift hour 6 to the actual sunrise and everything else accordingly.

It is also possible that the planetary hours in this Heptarchic scheme could follow a different rhythm, that of the planets as they occur within the structure of the system. That would make the flow Venus, Sol, Mars, Jupiter, Mercury, Saturn, Luna rather than Saturn, Jupiter, Mars, Sol, Venus, Mercury, Luna. But this is just food for thought. Such a rhythm would throw off the symmetry of the daily cycles. It works perfectly as is, and does not do so with the variation.

It should be kept in mind that the forty-two ministers of the princes rule during specific hours of the day and the night, which are based on the clock, and not calculated as above. Each minister rules a period of thirty-four minutes and seventeen seconds. Because of this, it may be more appropriate to view the planetary hours as based on clock time with these Heptarchic entities. I tend toward this way of operating personally. But I will leave this up to your experimentation. However you do your calculations, these beings offer the possibility of some fairly

---

[1] See *The New Hermetics Equinox Journal - Volume 1* for an alternate approach to calculating auspicious planetary days and hours.

nuanced magical work. In the next pages I will list the hierarchy for each day of the week, along with their sigils and talismans. It should be noted that the sigil for Bagenol might not be correct.

The Hierarchy of Sunday

Son of Light: Ilr
Son of the Son of Light: Ave

King: Bobogel (Sun)
Prince: Bornogo (Venus)

Governors:
Buscnab (Saturn)
Barnafa (Jupiter)
Bonefon (Mars)
Bariges (Mercury)
Bablibo (Moon)

The 42 Ministers for Prince Bornogo

12am-4am	LEENARB	EENARBL	ENARBLE	NARBLEE	ARBLEEN	RBLEENA	BLEENAR
4am-8am	LNANAEB	NANAEBL	AANEBLN	NAEBLNA	AEBLNAN	EBLNANA	BLNANAE
8am-12pm	ROEMNAB	OEMNABR	EMNABRO	MNABROE	NABROEM	ABROEMN	BROEMNA
12pm-4pm	LEAORIB	EAORIBL	AORIBLE	ORIBLEA	RIBLEAO	IBLEAOR	BLEAORI
4pm-8pm	NEICIAB	EICIAGN	ICIABNE	CIABNEI	IABNEIC	ABNEICI	BNEICIA
8pm-12am	AOIDIAB	OIDIABA	IDIABAO	DIABAOI	IABAOID	ABAOIDI	BAOIDIA

The Hierarchy of Monday

Son of Light: Stimcul
Son of the Son of Light: Ilemese

King: Blumaza (Moon)
Prince: Bralges (Saturn)

Governors:
Belmara (Jupiter)
Bragiop (Mars)
Brisfli (Sun)
Basledf (Venus)
Baspalo (Mercury)

The 42 Ministers for Prince Bralges

12am-4am	OESNGLE	ESNGLEO	SNGLEOE	NGLEOES	GLEOESN	LEOESNG	EOESNGL
4am-8am	AVZNILN	VZNILNA	ZNILNAV	NILNAVZ	ILNAVZN	LNAVZNI	NAVZNIL
8am-12pm	YLLMAFS	LLMAFSY	LMAFSYL	MAFSYLL	AFSYLLM	FSYLLMA	SYLLMAF
12pm-4pm	NRSOGOO	RSOGOON	SOGOONR	OGOONRS	GOONRSO	OONRSOG	ONRSOGO
4pm-8pm	NRRCPRN	RRCPRNN	RCPRNNR	CPRNNRR	PRNNRRC	RNNRRCP	NNRRCPR
8pm-12am	LABDGRE	ABDGREL	BDGRELA	DGRELAB	GRELABD	RELABDG	ELABDGR

O	E	S	N	G	L	E
A	V	Z	N	I	L	N
Y	L	L	M	A	F	S
N	R	S	O	G	O	O
N	R	R	C	P	R	N
L	A	B	D	G	R	E

230

The Hierarchy of Tuesday

Son of Light: Dmal
Son of the Son of Light: Liba

King: Babalel (Mars)
Prince: Befafes (Sun)

Governors:
Bminpol (Saturn)
Bmilges (Jupiter)
Bariges (Mercury)
Bapnido (Venus)
Busduna (Moon)

The 42 Ministers for Prince Befafes

12am-4am	EILOMFO	ILOMFOE	LOMFOEI	OMFOEIL	MFOEILO	FOEILOM	OEILOMF
4am-8am	NEOTPTA	EOTPTAN	OTPTANE	TPTANEO	PTANEOT	TANEOPT	ANEOTPT
8am-12pm	SAGACIY	AGACIYS	GACIYSA	ACIYSAG	CIYSAGA	IYSAGAC	YSAGACI
12pm-4pm	ONEDPON	NEDPONO	EDPONON	DPONONE	PONONED	ONONEDP	NONEDPO
4pm-8pm	NOONMAN	OONMANN	ONMANNO	NMANNOO	MANNOON	ANNOONM	NNOONMA
8pm-12am	ETEULGL	TEULGLE	EULGLET	ULGLETE	LGLETEU	GLETEUL	LETEULG

The Hierarchy of Wednesday

Son of Light: Ih
Son of the Son of Light: An

King: Bnaspol (Mercury)
Prince: Blisdon (Jupiter)

Governors:
Bliigan (Saturn)
Bazpama (Mars)
Bernole (Sun)
Blamapo (Venus)
Barfort (Moon)

The 42 Ministers for Prince Blisdon

12am-4am	ELGNSEB	LGNSEBE	GNSEBEL	NSEBELG	SEBELGN	EBELGNS	BELGNSE
4am-8am	NLINZVB	LINZVBN	INZVBNL	NZVBNLI	ZVBNLIN	VBNLINZ	BNLINZV
8am-12pm	SFAMLLB	FAMLLBS	AMLLBSF	MLLBSFA	LLBSFAM	LBSFAML	BSFAMLL
12pm-4pm	OOGOSRS	OGOSRSO	GOSRSOO	OSRSOOG	SRSOOGO	RSOOGOS	SOOGOSR
4pm-8pm	NRPCRRB	RPCRRBN	PCRRBNR	CRRBNRP	RRBNRPC	RBNRPCR	BNRPCRR
8pm-12am	ERGDBAB	RGDBABE	GDBABER	DBABERG	BABERGD	ABERGDB	BERGDBA

The Hierarchy of Thursday

Son of Light: Hecoa
Son of the Son of Light: Rocle

King: Bynepor (Jupiter)
Prince: Butmono (Mars)

Governors:
Bartiro (Saturn)
Basmelo (Sun)
Besgeme (Venus)
Baldago (Mercury)
Blingef (Moon)

The 42 Ministers for Prince Butmono

12am-4am	BBARNFL	BARNFLB	ARNFLBB	RNFLBBA	NFLBBAR	FLBBARN	LBBARNF
4am-8am	BBAIGAO	BAIGAOB	AIGAOBB	IGAOBBA	GAOBBAI	AOBBAIG	OBBAIGA
8am-12pm	BBALPAE	BALPAEB	ALPAEBB	LPAEBBA	PAEBBAL	AEBBALP	EBBALPA
12pm-4pm	BBANIFG	BANIFGB	ANIFGBB	NIFGBBA	IFGBBAN	FGBBANI	GBBANIF
4pm-8pm	BBOSNIA	BOSNIAB	OSNIABB	SNIABBO	NIABBOS	ISBBOSN	ABBOSNI
8pm-12am	BBASNOD	BASNODB	ASNODBB	SNODBBA	NODBBAS	ODBBASN	DBBASNO

The Hierarchy of Friday

Son of Light: I
Son of the Son of Light: El

King: Baligon (Venus)
Prince: Bagenol (Luna)

Governors:
Bormifa (Saturn)
Benpagi (Jupiter)
Bermale (Mars)
Bagnole (Sun)
Binodab (Mercury)

The 42 Ministers for Prince Bagenol

12am-4am	AOAYNNL	OAYNNLA	AYNNLAO	YNNLAOA	NNLAOAY	NLAOAYN	LAOAYNN
4am-8am	LBBNAAV	BBNAAVL	BNAAVLB	NAAVLBB	AAVLBBN	AVLBBNA	VLBBNAA
8am-12pm	IOAESPM	OAESPMI	AESPMIO	ESPMIOA	SPMIOAE	PMIOAES	MIOAESP
12pm-4pm	GGLPPSA	GLPPSAG	LPPSAGG	PPSAGGL	PSAGGLP	SAGGLPP	AGGLPPS
4pm-8pm	OEEOOEZ	EEOOEZO	EOOEZOE	OOEZOEE	OEZOEEO	EZOEEOO	ZOEEOOE
8pm-12am	NLLRLNA	LLRLNAN	LRLNANL	RLNANLL	LNANLLR	NANLLRL	ANLLRLN

A	O	A	Y	N	N	L
L	B	B	N	A	A	V
I	O	A	E	S	P	M
G	G	L	P	P	S	A
O	E	E	O	O	E	Z
N	L	L	R	L	N	A

The Hierarchy of Saturday

Son of Light: Beigia
Son of the Son of Light: Hagonel

King: Bnapsen (Saturn)
Prince: Brorges (Mercury)

Governors:
Buscnab (Jupiter)
Blintom (Mars)
Branglo (Sun)
Bmamgal (Venus)
Bamnode (Moon)

The 42 Ministers for Prince Brorges

12am-4am	BANSSZE	ANSSZEB	NSSZEBA	SSZEBAN	SZEBANS	ZEBANSS	EBANSSZ
4am-8am	BYAPARE	YAPAREB	APABEBY	PAREBYA	AREBYAP	REBYAPA	EBYAPAR
8am-12pm	BNAMGEN	NAMGENB	AMGENBN	MGENBNA	GENBNAM	ENBNAMG	NBNAMGE
12pm-4pm	BNVAGES	NVAGESB	VAGESBN	AGESBNV	GESBNVA	ESBNVAG	SBNVAGE
4pm-8pm	BLBOPOO	LBOPOOB	BOPOOBL	OPOOBLB	POOBLBO	OOBLBOP	OBLBOPO
8pm-12am	BABEPEN	ABEPENB	BEPENBA	EPENBAB	PENBABE	ENBABEP	NBABEPE

235

Chapter Sixteen
The Heptarchic Temple

In working with the heptarchic angels I highly recommend that you set up your temple with the holy table and the Sigillum Dei Aemeth. These symbols are intimately connected to the Heptarchia Mystica, and seem almost an essential part of the process of working with these beings. I cannot be certain of this, but I have never gotten good results without this set up.

The system of the 49 Heptarchical angels or the "Bonorum" was the first system of angels received by Dee and Kelly. These angels are much more closely related to the Sigillum Dei Aemeth and the Holy Table than the Watchtowers and Aethyrs. So, if you wish to work with this heptarchy you should probably try to make or obtain these symbolic instruments. These items are discussed in a little more detail in the appendices, though diagrams follow momentarily.

There are also two more pieces of ritual gear that you are supposed to possess. The Ring of Solomon and the Dee's Lamen. Both of these are reproduced at the end of this section. Lon Milo Duquette has occasionally suggested using a paper "Ring of Solomon" and I have found something like this (though not paper) perfectly effective myself. You might also be able to find a ring from some industrious jeweler on the internet or have one custom made if you are interested. The lamen can definitely be made from paper, framed in gold and worn on a golden chain.

Further, you will need three talismans for each day of the week.[1] The first talisman is the seal of ruling prince of the day. This is to be placed on the altar. The second talisman is a circular talisman with the seal of the daily king/son of son light on it. In Dee's original diaries, there is a complex cipher around this, but most of the cipher has been lost. I suggest that you place the circular table of the daily ministers around the seal, as in the above hierarchies. I have done so in my work with good results. This talisman is to be held in your hands throughout the invocation. The third talisman is the table of ministers. I use the square table from the hierarchies above, although some use the round table. All of these can be made from paper, or painted or glued onto wood. The original instructions call for "sweete wood.' These talismans can be present in your temple during the eighteen-day preliminary working and will be consecrated by their presence.

But do not allow the lack of perfect versions of any of these items prevent you from getting started. Find a suitable altern-ative and explore. Below are images of the key items of the temple.

---

[1] All of these talisman are printed in full color in the companion volume *The Enochian Magick Toolbook*. You can simply cut them out of this book and use them in your rituals. It also contains versions of the ring and lamen.

DIAGRAM 24 - THE HOLY TABLE

This is the basic design of the Holy Table. I will discuss it a bit further in Appendix D.

DIAGRAM 25 - THE SIGILLUM DEI AEMETH

The Sigillum Dei Aemeth or "Seal of God which is Truth" is to be made of pure wax, placed on the center of the table. Four smaller versions of the same seal are to be placed under the legs of the table. A red silk cloth is to be placed on top of it, with the shewtone set on top of the seal over the cloth. This set up insulates your whole work from all but pure influences. I will discuss the Sigillum Dei Aemeth a bit more in Appendix C.

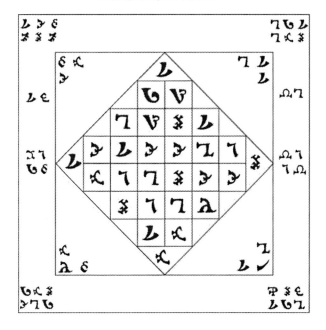

DIAGRAM 26 - THE LAMEN

This is the design of the lamen to be worn around your neck on a gold chain. The lamen should be four inches square.

DIAGRAM 27 - THE RING OF SOLOMON

This is the unique design of the Ring of Solomon delivered to Dee for use in Enochian work. It was said that without it nothing could be accomplished.

241

Chapter Seventeen
Practical Working Procedures

Working with the Heptarchic angels is quite similar to working with the Watchtower angels, and the reasons for doing so are largely the same, except that these angels are planetary in nature so you will use different openings. I will give complete examples of these openings in the next chapter. But you will use all of the same basic ritual techniques. Personally, I also use the First Enochian Key when I am invoking these beings, but your own experimentation will tell you whether it is helpful for you.

In setting up your temple you will need to place the table of ministers at the foot of your altar, so that you can stand on it when invoking. You will need to have the seal of the prince of the day on top of your altar, and have the round seal for the king at hand so that you can hold it during your invocations.

You can place the tables and seals for all the seven days around your altar if you wish, or just those of the specific day you are working. The orientation that I use for placing the tables is as follows. I also generally face these directions for the opening invocations.

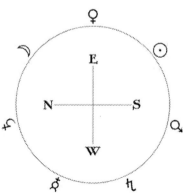

DIAGRAM 28 - HEPTARCHIC DIRECTIONS

This orientation creates a sevenfold "energy grid" in which the Sigillum Dei Aemeth, the Ensigns of Creation, the Tables of Ministers and your invocations are all spreading outward along the same lines from the center of your altar.

The following is a basic ritual outline for approaching Heptarchic workings. Although you will call upon the kings and princes in these ceremonies, I have personally found that the ministers are far easier to get into meaningful conversaion.

1. Enter the altered state through anchoring and deep breathing.

2. Make your inner temple conterminous with your physical workspace.

3. Generate Rosicrucian Love.

4. Perform the New Hermetics Grounding and Centering as a physical ritual.

5. Purify and consecrate circle.

6. State the purpose of your ritual.

7. Invoke cosmic consciousness.

8. Create a magical atmosphere appropriate to the planetary nature of your working.

9. Perform planetary invocation, (using ritual of the hexagram. You may vibrate the name of the Son of Light and the Son of the Son as you trace the hexagram).

10. (Here I usually vibrate the first Enochian key. I do this because it works for me. It is not a "traditional" part of the working procedure.)

11. Recite the invocation of the King and of the Prince.

[all of the above is contained in the Daily Rituals in the next chapter.]

12. Invoke the appropriate minister using Enochian (as in Part One, Chapter Seven (p. 141?).

13. Sit and enter altered state (if you have not done so previously).

14. (Here I again use my "image streaming" techniques. This is obviously optional). Allow the being to materialize in the atmosphere you have created. You may do this with eyes open or closed, or look into a crystal. (if you do this latter, concentrate all the invoked energy into the crystal which should be sitting atop your sigillum dei aemeth on your holy table).

15. Communicate with the being when it appears, conducting whatever work you will.

16. Give the being license to depart, thanking it for coming and getting assurances that you can communicate again in the future.

17. See its energy completely dissipating. Banish the planetary energy.

18. Perform the New Hermetics Grounding and Centering as a physical ritual.

19. Dedicate the Merit.

Chapter Eighteen
Daily Invitations to the Kings and Princes

The following simple rituals are the ones I use in working with the Heptarchia. They combine a New Hermetics planetary opening with modern adaptations of Dee's invocations from his original Heptarchia Mystica. As always, please feel free to edit and adjust these in any way for yourself. I am providing them to give you a framework in which to work, but your own words can be used to make the invocations more personal.

You will notice that the initial invocations are very planetary, but the actual invitations to the Royal personages are much more earthly. This expresses the nature of these beings as a whole quite well. They are angels who project planetary energies into our world.

In working with the Heptarchia, you will invoke the King and Prince of the day even if you are intending to work with another minister or governor.

Sunday

Your temple should be set up with Holy Table and Sigillum Dei Aemeth. The appropriate talismanic square of daily ministers should be at the foot of your table, and the talismanic circle of ministers should be on the altar, along with the seal of the Prince. You will need to be wearing the Lamen and Ring, and have your wand available.

Sit in your temple and enter the altered state. Use your powers of visualization to make your Inner Temple conterminous with the room

or temple in which you are physically sitting, (or else merely visualize that you are in both places at once).

Begin by Generating Rosicrucian Love.

Perform the New Hermetics Grounding & Centering ritual.

Purify and consecrate your workspace.

Knock once on top of your altar.

Invoke Cosmic Consciousness, saying:

"Supreme consciousness of the universe, of which my greatest conceptions are but a tiny spark, with which and from which I seek communion and knowledge, unfathomable self of all, I seek this day to be brought into the knowledge and communication of those facets of your infinite intelligence that reveal your limitless glory in a sevenfold manner under the name of the mystical heptarchy. It is my will to commune with these good angels, these messengers of divine authority so that I may increase my knowledge and assist in whatever small way I can with the continuing evolution and perfection of the universe. I seek only to perfect myself, so that I may be of service in the positive growth and transformation of created existence. Place me in contact with your good counselors, so that by their offices in seven-fold division according to each of their virtues and powers I may increase the presence of the divine in my life and in the lives of all living beings with whom I connect. Let me always enjoy the friendly conversation and communion with your spiritual messengers, and most particularly those of the mystical heptarchy. Let this be accomplished by my will, which is one with your will. *(vibrate)* AUM AUM AUM."

Knock once.

[Throughout the following use pore breathing and projecting energy to accumulate the Solar force.]

Go to the Solar edge of your circle and face outward, visualizing the golden orange orb of the Sun blazing in front of you, saying:

"Spirits of the Sun, powers of the great light of the firmament, be with me. Let your harmonious golden orange rays bring balance and wholeness to this rite. As all things revolve about the sun, let this circle be a receptacle of divine power, illumination, prosperity and peace. There is healing in this light, and the joy of youth. Spirits of the Sun, I invoke you."

Make the sign of Rending the Veil, saying:

"By *(vibrate names)* RAPHAEL and SEMELIEL I open and activate my communication with the spirits of the Sun."

Take up your Wand in your dominant hand, and the Heptarchic Talisman in other hand.

Make the first three Invoking Hexagrams of Sol, vibrating:

"ILR."

Make the second three Invoking Hexagrams of Sol, vibrating:

"AVE"

Say, "The Spirits of the Sun are invoked!"

Knock: 333 --- 22 --- 333 --- 333 --- 22 --- 333

[Here you can vibrate the first key (Ol Sonf Vorsg...) If you choose to do so]

249

Say, "O Powerful and Noble King BOBOGEL, And by any other names by which you may be known, who rules over the distributing, giving and bestowing of wisdom and knowledge, the teaching of true philosophy, true understanding of all learning, grounded upon wisdom, and of many other great mysteries. In the Name of the supreme consciousness of the universe, creator of all things visible and invisible: O Noble King BOBOGEL come, now, and appear, with your Prince, and his Ministers and Subjects, visible to my eyes in beautiful form, to assist me in advancing in the light of cosmic consciousness and to help in the advancement and evolution of the whole universe through your wisdom and power. AUM. COME, Noble King BOBOGEL I say COME. AUM."

Say, "O Noble Prince BORNOGO, And by any other names by which you may be known, whose princely office oversees the perfecting of corrupted nature, the knowledge of metals, and Generally the Princely Ministering to the Noble and Mighty King BOBOGEL, in his government of Distributing, giving and bestowing of Wisdom, knowledge, True Philosophy, and true understanding of all learning grounded upon Wisdom. In the Name of the supreme consciousness of the universe, creator of all things visible and invisible: I need you noble Prince BORNOGO to come presently, visibly to my eyes in beautiful form, with your Ministers and Subjects, to assist me in advancing in the light of cosmic consciousness and to help in the advancement and evolution of the whole universe through your wisdom and power. AUM. COME, Noble Prince BORNOGO I say COME. AUM."

Invoke the appropriate minister.

Monday

Your temple should be set up with Holy Table and Sigillum Dei Aemeth. The appropriate talismanic square of daily ministers should be at the foot of your table, and the talismanic circle of ministers should be on the altar, along with the seal of the Prince. You will need to be wearing the Lamen and Ring, and have your wand available.

Sit in your temple and enter the altered state. Use your powers of visualization to make your Inner Temple conterminous with the room or temple in which you are physically sitting, (or else merely visualize that you are in both places at once).

Begin by Generating Rosicrucian Love.

Perform the New Hermetics Grounding & Centering ritual.

Purify and consecrate your workspace.

Knock once on top of your altar.

Invoke Cosmic Consciousness, saying:

"Supreme consciousness of the universe, of which my greatest conceptions are but a tiny spark, with which and from which I seek communion and knowledge, unfathomable self of all, I seek this day to be brought into the knowledge and communication of those facets of your infinite intelligence that reveal your limitless glory in a sevenfold manner under the name of the mystical heptarchy. It is my will to commune with these good angels, these messengers of divine authority so that I may increase my knowledge and assist in whatever small way I can with the continuing evolution and perfection of the universe. I seek only to perfect myself, so that I may be of service in the positive growth and transformation of created existence. Place me in contact with your good counselors, so that by their offices in seven-fold division according to each of their virtues and powers I may increase the presence of the divine in my life and in the lives of all living beings with whom I connect. Let me always enjoy the friendly conversation and communion with your spiritual messengers, and most particularly those of the mystical heptarchy. Let this be accomplished by my will, which is one with your will. *(vibrate)* AUM AUM AUM."

Knock once.

[Throughout the following use pore breathing and projecting energy to accumulate the Lunar force.]

Go to the Lunar edge of your circle and face outward, visualizing the blue-white orb of the Moon blazing in front of you, saying:

"Spirits of the Moon, powers of the second light, be with me. Let your dreamy blue rays bring clairvoyant images and imagination to this rite. Powers of the subconscious tides, even of the tides of the great deep, let this circle be a receptacle of the astral light, awakening the powers of emotion and instinct to flow like the sea. Spirits of the Moon, I invoke you."

Make the sign of Rending the Veil, saying:

"By GABRIEL and LEVANAEL I open and activate my communication with the spirits of the Moon."

Take up the Wand in your dominant hand, and the Heptarchic Talisman in other hand.

Make the first triangle of the Invoking Hexagram of the Moon, vibrating:

"STIMCUL"

Make the second triangle of the Invoking Hexagram of the Moon, vibrating:

"ILEMESE"

Say, "The Spirits of the Moon are invoked!"

Knock: 333 --- 1 --- 333 --- 1 --- 333

[Here you can vibrate the first key (Ol Sonf Vorsg...) *If you choose to do so]*

Say, "O Powerful and Noble King BLUMAZA And by any other names by which you may be known, who rules over discovering the divine mysteries, the understanding of all knowledge past, present and future, in the Name of the supreme consciousness of the universe, creator of all things visible and invisible: O Noble King BLUMAZA Come, Now, and Appear, with your Prince, and his Ministers and Subjects, visible to my eyes in beautiful form, to assist me in advancing in the light of cosmic consciousness and to help in the advancement and evolution of the whole universe through your wisdom and power. AUM. COME, Noble King BLUMAZA I say COME. AUM."

Say, "O Noble Prince, BRALGES And by any other names by which you may be known, whose princely office oversees the aerial invisible creatures living in your dominion, Who said, "Behold, I am Come: I will teach the Names without Numbers. The Creatures subject unto me, shall be known unto you." In the Name of the supreme consciousness of the universe, creator of all things visible and invisible: I need you noble Prince BRALGES to come presently visibly to my eyes in beautiful form, with your Ministers and Subjects, to assist me in advancing in the light of cosmic consciousness and to help in the advancement and evolution of the whole universe through your wisdom and power. AUM. COME, Noble Prince BRALGES I say COME. AUM."

Invoke the appropriate minister.

Tuesday

Your temple should be set up with Holy Table and Sigillum Dei Aemeth. The appropriate talismanic square of daily ministers should be at the foot of your table, and the talismanic circle of ministers should be on the altar, along with the seal of the Prince. You will need to be wearing the Lamen and Ring, and have your wand available.

Sit in your temple and enter the altered state. Use your powers of visualization to make your Inner Temple conterminous with the room or temple in which you are physically sitting, (or else merely visualize that you are in both places at once).

Begin by Generating Rosicrucian Love.

Perform the New Hermetics Grounding & Centering ritual.

Purify and consecrate your workspace.

Knock once on top of your altar.

Invoke Cosmic Consciousness, saying:

"Supreme consciousness of the universe, of which my greatest conceptions are but a tiny spark, with which and from which I seek communion and knowledge, unfathomable self of all, I seek this day to be brought into the knowledge and communication of those facets of your infinite intelligence that reveal your limitless glory in a sevenfold manner under the name of the mystical heptarchy. It is my will to commune with these good angels, these messengers of divine authority so that I may increase my knowledge and assist in whatever small way I can with the continuing evolution and perfection of the universe. I seek only to perfect myself, so that I may be of service in the positive growth and transformation of created existence. Place me in contact with your good counselors, so that by their offices in seven-fold division according to each of their virtues and powers I may increase the presence of the divine in my life and in the lives of all living beings with whom I connect. Let me always enjoy the friendly conversation and communion with your spiritual messengers, and most particularly those of the mystical heptarchy. Let this be accomplished by my will, which is one with your will. *(vibrate)* AUM AUM AUM."

Knock once.

[Throughout the following use pore breathing and projecting energy to accumulate the Martial force.]

Go to the Martial edge of your circle and face outward, visualizing the flaming red orb of Mars blazing in front of you, saying:

"Spirits of Mars, powers of the fiery red light, be with me. Let your scarlet rays bring force and energy to this rite. Let the might of war charge my temple with vigor and masculine power, the red blood of nature's pulse spilling in the frenzy of destruction and justice. Let this circle be a receptacle of aggression, the power of battle and competition to rend and tear, that violence and athletic might will prevail in this hour of strength. Spirits of Mars, I invoke you."

Make the sign of Rending the Veil, saying:

"By CUMAEL and MADIMIEL I open and activate my communication with the spirits of Mars."

Take up the Wand in your dominant hand, and the Heptarchic Talisman in other hand.

Make the first triangle of the Invoking Hexagram of Mars, vibrating:

"DMAL"

Make the second triangle of the Invoking Hexagram of Mars, vibrating:

"LIBA"

Say, "The Spirits of Mars are invoked!"

Knock: 333 --- 55555 --- 333

[Here you can vibrate the first key (Ol Sonf Vorsg…) *If you choose to do so]*

Say, "O Powerful and Noble King BABALEL and by any other names by which you may be known, who rules as King in the waters, mighty and wonderful in waters, whose power is in the bowels of the waters, whose royal person with your Noble Prince BEFAFES, and his 42 Ministers, The Triple Crowned King CARMARA bade be used to the glory of the almighty, therefore in the Name of the supreme consciousness of the universe, creator of all things visible and invisible: O Noble King BABALEL Come, Now, and Appear, with your Prince, and his Ministers and Subjects, visible to my eyes in beautiful form, to assist me in advancing in the light of cosmic consciousness and to help in the advancement and evolution of the whole universe through your wisdom and power. AUM. COME, Noble King BABALEL I say COME. AUM."

Say, "O Noble Prince, BEFAFES And by any other names by which you may be known, who is Prince of the Seas, your power is upon the waters. It was you who drowned the Pharaoh and your name was known to Moses. You were with King Solomon, you were called OBELISON amongst the Egyptians, in respect of your pleasant deliverance, whose 42 noble ministers have great power and authority- some in the measuring of the motions of the waters, and saltiness of the seas, some in giving good success in battles, reducing ships, and all manner of vessels upon the seas, some over all the fishes and monsters of the seas, and generally, are the distributers of the supreme Judgments upon the Waters, while others beautify Nature in her Composition. while the rest are distributors and deliverers of the treasures and unknown substances of the Seas. In the Name of the supreme consciousness of the universe, creator of all things visible and invisible: I need you noble Prince BEFAFES to come presently visibly to my eyes in beautiful form, with your Ministers and Subjects, to assist me in advancing in the light of cosmic consciousness and to help in the advancement and evolution of the whole universe through your wisdom and power. AUM. COME, Noble Prince BEFAFES I say COME. AUM."

Invoke the appropriate minister.

Wednesday

Your temple should be set up with Holy Table and Sigillum Dei Aemeth. The appropriate talismanic square of daily ministers should be at the foot of your table, and the talismanic circle of ministers should be on the altar, along with the seal of the Prince. You will need to be wearing the Lamen and Ring, and have your wand available.

Sit in your temple and enter the altered state. Use your powers of visualization to make your Inner Temple conterminous with the room or temple in which you are physically sitting, (or else merely visualize that you are in both places at once).

Begin by Generating Rosicrucian Love.

Perform the New Hermetics Grounding & Centering ritual.

Purify and consecrate your workspace.

Knock once on top of your altar.

Invoke Cosmic Consciousness, saying:

"Supreme consciousness of the universe, of which my greatest conceptions are but a tiny spark, with which and from which I seek communion and knowledge, unfathomable self of all, I seek this day to be brought into the knowledge and communication of those facets of your infinite intelligence that reveal your limitless glory in a sevenfold manner under the name of the mystical heptarchy. It is my will to commune with these good angels, these messengers of divine authority so that I may increase my knowledge and assist in whatever small way I can with the continuing evolution and perfection of the universe. I seek only to perfect myself, so that I may be of service in the positive growth and transformation of created existence. Place me in contact with your good counselors, so that by their offices in seven-fold division according to each of their virtues and powers I may increase the presence of the divine in my life and in the lives of all living beings with whom I connect. Let me always enjoy the friendly conversation and communion with your spiritual messengers, and most particularly those of the mystical heptarchy. Let this be accomplished by my will, which is one with your will. *(vibrate)* AUM AUM AUM."

Knock once.

[Throughout the following use pore breathing and projecting energy to accumulate the Mercurial force.]

Go to the Mercurial edge of your circle and face outward, visualizing the yellow-white orb of Mercury blazing in front of you with shifting colors, saying:

"Spirits of Mercury, powers of the intellectual light, be with me. Let your changeable rays bring flexibility and mental agility to this rite. Let the principles of universal order bring the light of reason to charge my temple with the power of logic and communication. May sweet words be on my tongue and in my writing instruments to bring greater knowledge into this world through mathematics, rhetoric and all the liberal sciences. Let this circle be a receptacle of the medicine of the mind, traveling to the farthest reaches of infinite wisdom. Spirits of Mercury, I invoke you."

Make the sign of Rending the Veil, saying:

"By MICHAEL and CORABIEL I open and activate my communication with the spirits of Mercury."

Take up the Wand in your dominant hand, and the Heptarchic Talisman in other hand.

Make the first triangle of the Invoking Hexagram of Mercury vibrating:

"IH"

Make the second triangle of the Invoking Hexagram of Mercury vibrating:

"AN"

Say, "The Spirits of Mercury are invoked!"

Knock: 4444 --- 333 --- 4444

[Here you can vibrate the first key (Ol Sonf Vorsg...) If you choose to do so]

Say, "O Powerful and Noble King BNASPOL And by any other names by which you may be known, who rules over the Earth with her bowels, and to whom the secrets of the Earth whatsoever are delivered, in the Name of the supreme consciousness of the universe, creator of all things visible and invisible: O Noble King BNASPOL Come, Now, and Appear, with your Prince, and his Ministers and Subjects, visible to my eyes in beautiful form, to assist me in advancing in the light of cosmic consciousness and to help in the advancement and evolution of the whole universe through your wisdom and power. AUM. COME, Noble King BNASPOL I say COME. AUM."

Say, "O Noble Prince, BLISDON And by any other names by which you may be known, unto whom the keys of the mysteries of the Earth, are delivered, whose 42 Ministers are Angels that govern under thee. All of whom thy Mighty King BNASPOL has willed to be used, and affirmed that they are, and shall be, at my Command, in the Name of the supreme consciousness of the universe, creator of all things visible and invisible: I need you noble Prince BLISDON to come presently visibly to my eyes in beautiful form, with your Ministers and Subjects, to assist me in advancing in the light of cosmic consciousness and to help in the advancement and evolution of the whole universe through your wisdom and power. AUM. COME, Noble Prince BLISDON I say COME. AUM."

Invoke the appropriate minister.

Thursday

Your temple should be set up with Holy Table and Sigillum Dei Aemeth. The appropriate talismanic square of daily ministers should be at the foot of your table, and the talismanic circle of ministers should be on the altar, along with the seal of the Prince. You will need to be wearing the Lamen and Ring, and have your wand available.

Sit in your temple and enter the altered state. Use your powers of visualization to make your Inner Temple conterminous with the room

260

or temple in which you are physically sitting, (or else merely visualize that you are in both places at once).

Begin by Generating Rosicrucian Love.

Perform the New Hermetics Grounding & Centering ritual.

Purify and consecrate your workspace.

Knock once on top of your altar.

Invoke Cosmic Consciousness, saying:

"Supreme consciousness of the universe, of which my greatest conceptions are but a tiny spark, with which and from which I seek communion and knowledge, unfathomable self of all, I seek this day to be brought into the knowledge and communication of those facets of your infinite intelligence that reveal your limitless glory in a sevenfold manner under the name of the mystical heptarchy. It is my will to commune with these good angels, these messengers of divine authority so that I may increase my knowledge and assist in whatever small way I can with the continuing evolution and perfection of the universe. I seek only to perfect myself, so that I may be of service in the positive growth and transformation of created existence. Place me in contact with your good counselors, so that by their offices in seven-fold division according to each of their virtues and powers I may increase the presence of the divine in my life and in the lives of all living beings with whom I connect. Let me always enjoy the friendly conversation and communion with your spiritual messengers, and most particularly those of the mystical heptarchy. Let this be accomplished by my will, which is one with your will. *(vibrate)* AUM AUM AUM."

Knock once.

[Throughout the following use pore breathing and projecting energy to accumulate the Jupiterean force.]

Go to the Jupiterean edge of your circle and face outward, visualizing the violet orb of Jupiter blazing in front of you, saying:

"Spirits of Jupiter, powers of the Jovian light, be with me. Let your expansive rays bring abundance, wealth and position to this rite. May honor and dignity be bestowed upon this temple through the power of abundance and prosperity. Bring good fortune and divine providence to all matters of societal order, through your powers of leadership, your visionary insights and majestic grace. Spirits of Jupiter, I invoke you."

Make the sign of Rending the Veil, saying:

"By ZADKIEL and ZEDEKIEL I open and activate my communication with the spirits of Jupiter."

Take up the Wand in your dominant hand, and the Heptarchic Talisman in other hand.

Make the first triangle of the Invoking Hexagram of Jupiter, vibrating:

"HEEOA"

Make the second triangle of the Invoking Hexagram of Jupiter, vibrating:

"ROCLE"

Say, "The Spirits of Jupiter are invoked!"

Knock: 22 --- 333 --- 1 --- 333 --- 22

[Here you can vibrate the first key (Ol Sonf Vorsg…) if you choose to do so]

Say, "O Powerful and Noble King BYNEPOR And by any other names by which you may be known, who rules over the general state and condition of all things, whose glory and renown is never ending, you are the very force of godhead, manifesting all things, in the name of the supreme consciousness, you are in all, and all has some being by you, you begin new worlds, new people, new kings, and new knowledge of a new government, in the Name of the supreme consciousness of the universe, creator of all things visible and invisible: O Noble King BYNEPOR Come, Now, and Appear, with your Prince, and his Ministers and Subjects, visible to my eyes in beautiful form, to assist me in advancing in the light of cosmic consciousness and to help in the advancement and evolution of the whole universe through your wisdom and power. AUM. COME, Noble King BYNEPOR I say COME. AUM."

Say, "O Noble Prince, BVTMONO And by any other names by which you may be known, whose princely office oversees life and breath in living Creatures, all things live through your power, you bring life to all the kinds of creatures of the Earth, your seal is their glory, you know the hours of birth, life and death of all creatures, and administer each of these, in the name of the supreme consciousness of the universe, creator of all things visible and invisible: I need you noble Prince BVTMONO to come presently visibly to my eyes in beautiful form, with your Ministers and Subjects, to assist me in advancing in the light of cosmic consciousness and to help in the advancement and evolution of the whole universe through your wisdom and power. AUM. COME, Noble Prince BVTMONO I say COME. AUM."

Invoke the appropriate minister.

friday

Your temple should be set up with Holy Table and Sigillum Dei Aemeth. The appropriate talismanic square of daily ministers should be at the foot of your table, and the talismanic circle of ministers should be on the altar, along with the seal of the Prince. You will need to be wearing the Lamen and Ring, and have your wand available.

Sit in your temple and enter the altered state. Use your powers of visualization to make your Inner Temple conterminous with the room or temple in which you are physically sitting, (or else merely visualize that you are in both places at once).

Begin by Generating Rosicrucian Love.

Perform the New Hermetics Grounding & Centering ritual.

Purify and consecrate your workspace.

Knock once on top of your altar.

Invoke Cosmic Consciousness, saying:

"Supreme consciousness of the universe, of which my greatest conceptions are but a tiny spark, with which and from which I seek communion and knowledge, unfathomable self of all, I seek this day to be brought into the knowledge and communication of those facets of your infinite intelligence that reveal your limitless glory in a sevenfold manner under the name of the mystical heptarchy. It is my will to commune with these good angels, these messengers of divine authority so that I may increase my knowledge and assist in whatever small way I can with the continuing evolution and perfection of the universe. I seek only to perfect myself, so that I may be of service in the positive growth and transformation of created existence. Place me in contact with your good counselors, so that by their offices in seven-fold division according to each of their virtues and powers I may increase the presence of the divine in my life and in the lives of all living beings with whom I connect. Let me always enjoy the friendly conversation and communion with your spiritual messengers, and most particularly those of the mystical heptarchy. Let this be accomplished by my will, which is one with your will. *(vibrate)* AUM AUM AUM."

Knock once.

[Throughout the following use pore breathing and projecting energy to accumulate the Venusian force.]

Go to the Venusian edge of your circle and face outward, visualizing the emerald green orb of Venus blazing in front of you, saying:

"Spirits of Venus, powers of the lovely star, be with me. Let your green-hued rays of life and love bring beauty and pleasure to this rite. Nurture this temple with the divine feminine force, let the sweet scent of love fill the world. Let this circle be a receptacle of desire and pleasure, luxury and delight. Bring creativity, artistry and aesthetic perfection in this hour of love. Spirits of Venus, I invoke you."

Make the sign of Rending the Veil, saying:

"By HANIEL and NOGAHEL I open and activate my communication with the spirits of Venus."

Take up the Wand in your dominant hand, and the Heptarchic Talisman in other hand.

Make the first triangle of the Invoking Hexagram of Venus, vibrating:

"I"

Make the second triangle of the Invoking Hexagram of Venus, vibrating:

"EL"

Say, "The Spirits of Venus are invoked!"

Knock: 333 --- 22 --- 1 --- 22 --- 333

[Here you can vibrate the first key (Ol Sonf Vorsg…) *If you choose to do so]*

Say, "O Powerful and Noble King BALIGON and by any other names by which you may be known, who distributes and bestows at pleasure all that can be wrought in aerial Actions, and who has the government of yourself perfectly as a mystery known unto yourself, in the Name of the supreme consciousness of the universe, creator of all things visible and invisible: O Noble King BALIGON Come, Now, and Appear, with your Prince, and his Ministers and Subjects, visible to my eyes in beautiful form, to assist me in advancing in the light of cosmic consciousness and to help in the advancement and evolution of the whole universe through your wisdom and power. AUM. COME, Noble King BALIGON I say COME. AUM."

Say, "O Noble Prince, BAGENOL and by any other names by which you may be known, whose princely office oversees your own unique royal properties, and Generally the Princely Ministering to the Noble and Mighty King BALIGON in his government, in the Name of the supreme consciousness of the universe, creator of all things visible and invisible: I need you noble Prince BAGENOL to come presently visibly to my eyes in beautiful form, with your Ministers and Subjects, to assist me in advancing in the light of cosmic consciousness and to help in the advancement and evolution of the whole universe through your wisdom and power. AUM. COME, Noble Prince BAGENOL I say COME. AUM."

Invoke the appropriate minister.

Saturday

Your temple should be set up with Holy Table and Sigillum Dei Aemeth. The appropriate talismanic square of daily ministers should be at the foot of your table, and the talismanic circle of ministers should be on the altar, along with the seal of the Prince. You will need to be wearing the Lamen and Ring, and have your wand available.

Sit in your temple and enter the altered state. Use your powers of visualization to make your Inner Temple conterminous with the room or temple in which you are physically sitting, (or else merely visualize that you are in both places at once).

Begin by Generating Rosicrucian Love.

Perform the New Hermetics Grounding & Centering ritual.

Purify and consecrate your workspace.

Knock once on top of your altar.

Invoke Cosmic Consciousness, saying:

"Supreme consciousness of the universe, of which my greatest conceptions are but a tiny spark, with which and from which I seek communion and knowledge, unfathomable self of all, I seek this day to be brought into the knowledge and communication of those facets of your infinite intelligence that reveal your limitless glory in a sevenfold manner under the name of the mystical heptarchy. It is my will to commune with these good angels, these messengers of divine authority so that I may increase my knowledge and assist in whatever small way I can with the continuing evolution and perfection of the universe. I seek only to perfect myself, so that I may be of service in the positive growth and transformation of created existence. Place me in contact with your good counselors, so that by their offices in seven-fold division according to each of their virtues and powers I may increase the presence of the divine in my life and in the lives of all living beings with whom I connect. Let me always enjoy the friendly conversation and communion with your spiritual messengers, and most particularly those of the mystical heptarchy. Let this be accomplished by my will, which is one with your will. *(vibrate)* AUM AUM AUM."

Knock once.

[Throughout the following use pore breathing and projecting energy to accumulate the Saturnian force.]

Go to the Saturnian edge of your circle and face outward, visualizing the indigo orb of Saturn blazing in front of you, saying:

"Spirits of Saturn, powers of the ancient one, be with me. Let your indigo rays of mystery and darkness bring the deep structures of the matrix of creation to this rite. Bring the power of understanding the cycles of life and of death to this temple. Let your seriousness, heaviness and limitation bring responsibility, making this circle a receptacle of structure, understanding and the archetypes of the great void beyond in this hour of darkness and death. Spirits of Saturn, I invoke you."

Make the sign of Rending the Veil, saying:

"By ZAPHKIEL and SABATHIEL I open and activate my communication with the spirits of Saturn."

Take up the Wand in your dominant hand, and the Heptarchic Talisman in other hand.

Make the first triangle of the Invoking Hexagram of Saturn, vibrating:

"BEIGIA"

Make the second triangle of the Invoking Hexagram of Saturn, vibrating:

"HAGONEL"

Say, "The Spirits of Saturn are invoked!"

Knock: 4444 --- 1 --- 1 --- 1 --- 4444

[Here you can vibrate the first key (Ol Sonf Vorsg...) if you choose to do so]

Say, "O Powerful and Noble King BNAPSEN And by any other names by which you may be known, who rules over casting out the power of all wicked spirits, and giving knowledge of the actions and practices of evil men, and more than may be spoken or uttered to man, in the Name of the supreme consciousness of the universe, creator of all things visible and invisible: O Noble King BNAPSEN Come, Now, and Appear, with your Prince, and his Ministers and Subjects, visible to my eyes in beautiful form, to assist me in advancing in the light of cosmic consciousness and to help in the advancement and evolution of the whole universe through your wisdom and power. AUM. COME, Noble King BNAPSEN I say COME. AUM."

Say, "O Noble Prince, BRORGES And by any other names by which you may be known, who, being the Prince, chief Minister, and Governour under the great king BNAPSEN, has appeared in a most terrible manner with fiery flaming streams. In the Name of the supreme consciousness of the universe, creator of all things visible and invisible: I need you noble Prince BRORGES to come presently visibly to my eyes in beautiful form, with your Ministers and Subjects, to assist me in advancing in the light of cosmic consciousness and to help in the advancement and evolution of the whole universe through your wisdom and power. AUM. COME, Noble Prince BRORGES I say COME. AUM."

Invoke the appropriate minister.

Appendix A
The Forty-Nine Enochian Keys

Probably the most well known part of Enochian Magick is the set of 49 Keys or calls. These are a series of beautiful and poetic invocations given in the mysterious language often called either Enochian or Angelic. The interesting thing about these calls is that their actual purpose is never made clear in Dee's diaries. The Golden Dawn made a noble effort to assign these keys to the watchtowers, but this assignment does not come directly from Dee. In fact, it seems in all likelihood that the keys are not actually needed to invoke the angels of the watchtowers or most of the other beings in this book, at least not according to Dee's magical notebooks. Nonetheless I have continued to use them in this manual largely in the manner of the Golden Dawn. One reason for this is because the sonorous nature of the keys puts one into a state that facilitates visionary work. They have also been used successfully in this manner for well over a century if not far longer. Their use certainly does not hinder Enochian invocation, and seems helpful. If the angels reveal a different use for the keys to you, by all means experiment with that suggestion.

This angelic language, and all of the names and words from the Enochian system have a unique twenty one letter alphabet.

A		"Un"
B		"Pa"
C, K		"Veh"
D		"Gal"
E		"Graph"
F		"Fam"

271

G	𝕭	"Ged"
H	ℭ	"Na"
I, J, Y	𝟕	"Gon"
L	𝓧	"Ur"
M	ℰ	"Tal"
N	𝔂	"Drux"
O	𝓛	"Med"
P	ℳ	"Mals"
Q	𝓤	"Ger"
R	ℰ	"Don"
S	𝟏	"Fam"
T	✓	"Gisg"
U, V, W	𝕒	"Van"
X	𝓖	"Pal"
Z	𝕻	"Ceph"

While this book contains mostly the Roman alphabet, and it is not absolutely necessary to fully memorize the Enochian alphabet in order to start working with this system, it should be remembered that the Enochian language is essentially talismanic. Just as in the Hebrew qabala, each letter has a sort of power of its own, and it is this that we are calling upon with the Enochian keys and the names of the angels. I say this with confidence because there are several different popular methods of pronouncing the Enochian language, and they all "work." The magick is in the letters themselves, with pronunciation seemingly a secondary affair, at least practically speaking.

Generally, I do not personally use the Golden Dawn method of pronunciation, as it turns nearly every Enochian word into a long, ridiculously complicated mouthful. Instead, I simply pronounce words phonetically, adding the occasional vowel sound where necessary in long strings of consonants. The following rules of thumb for pronunciation should be helpful, although there are other pronunciation methods that you may also find effective. Nonetheless, this is the way that I pronounce Enochian, and it seems quite acceptable to the angels:

A	"Ah"
E	"Ay"
I	"Ee"
O	"Oh"
U	"Oo"

C	hard as in "K"
G	can be hard or soft
Q	can be pronounced "Kw" or "K"

There are in fact only nineteen different "keys" in this appendix. According to the angels, the actual first key is so holy that it is never pronounced. So, what we call "The First Key" is actually the second key by divine reckoning. The nineteenth key that opens the aethyrs forms the last thirty keys by varying the name of the aethyr you are working with, making a total of forty-nine keys. The use of the keys in this book is based for the most part on the associations of the Golden Dawn, with a few variations suggested by other magicians and my interactions with the Angels. There are other possible assignments, and it may also be possible to use these calls entirely on their own for some other purpose than invoking the angels presented in this book. You will have to experiment for yourself.

In presenting these keys I have consulted both Sloane Manuscript 3191 and the Cotton Appendix from the British Museum. I have also consulted secondary sources such as Geoffrey James's *The Enochian Magick of John Dee (Enochian Evocation)*, Meric Casaubon's *A True and Faithful Relation...* and Aleister Crowley's *Equinox, Vol. 1, Nos. 7 and 8*. There are vast discrepencies amongst these sources, even within the two manuscripts in Dee's own hand.

I have been forced to make editorial decisions in many places and have tried to go with words and passages that seem to make the most sense out of the language (from my very limited under-standing). It should be noted that many magicians have success-fully used quite corrupt versions of these keys for practical mag-ick, so there definitely seems to be some latitude. Apologies for any glaring errors that may have crept in along the way.

The phonetic pronunciation guide that follows each key is just my interpretation. There are numerous other possibilities. My feeling is that you should pronounce this language in the way that makes it most powerfully "magical" for you. What that means exactly will be something you need to figure out through experimentation. Certainly discovering how best to "vibrate" the language will be the first step. Performing the eighteen-day pre-liminary operation will allow you to work with several of these keys many times. Take this opportunity to experiment.

The First Key
Invokes the whole Tablet of Union
General Enochian Opening

ROMAN CHARACTERS:

Ol sonf vorsg goho Iad balt lansh calz vonpho sobra zol ror i ta Nazpsad Graa ta Malprg Ds holq Qaa nothoa zimz Od commah ta nobloh zien Soba thil gnonp prge aldi Ds urbs oboleh grsam Casarm ohorela caba pir Ds zonrensg cab erm Iadnah Pilah farzm znrza adna od gono Iadpil Ds hom Od toh Soba iaod Ipam Od ul Ipamis Ds loholo vep zomd Poamal Od bogpa aai ta piap piamol od vaoan ZACARe ca od ZAMRAN Odo cicle Qaa Zorge Lap zirdo Noco MAD Hoath Iaida

PHONETIC:

OL SONF VORS-JUH GOHO EE-YAD BALT LANSH CALZ VONFO SOBRA ZOL ROR EE TA NAZ-PUH-SAD GRAH-AH TAH MALPURJ DES HOL-KWUH KWUH-AH-AH NO-THO-AH ZEEMZ OD COM-MAH TA NOBLOH ZEE-EN SOBA THEEL GUH-NON-PUH PURJ ALDEE DES YOORBS O-BO-LAY GURSAM KASARM OHO-RAY-LA KABA PEER DES

274

ZON-RENS-JUH KAB ERM EE-YAD-NAH PUH-EE-LAH FAR-ZUM ZNUR-
ZAH ADNA OD GONO EE-AD-PEEL DES HOM OD TOH, SOBA EE-YAH-
OD EE-PAM OD YOOL EE-PAM-EES DES LOHOLO VEP ZOMD PO-AH-
MAL OD BOGPA AH-AH-EE TA PEE-AP PEE-AH-MAH-EL OD VA-OH-
AN ZAKAR-AY KUH-AH OD ZAMRAN ODO KEE-KLAY KWUH-AH-AH
ZORJ LAP ZEER-DO NOKO MAD HO-ATH EE-YAH-EE-DAH

ENGLISH TRANSLATION:

I reign over you, saith the God of Justice, in power exalted above
the Firmament of Wrath, in whose hands the Sun is as a sword,
and the Moon as a through-thrusting Fire: which measureth
your garments in the midst of my vestures, and trussed you
together as the palms of my hands: Whose seats I garnished with
the fire of gathering, and beautified your garments with admir-
ation, to whom I made a law to govern the Holy Ones, and delivered ye a Rod, with the Ark of Knowledge. Moreover you lift-
ed up your voices and sware obedience and faith to him that
liveth and triumpheth, whose beginning is not nor end cannot
be: which shineth as a flame in the midst of your palace and
reigneth amongst you as the balance of righteousness, and truth:
Move therefore, and shew yourselves: Open the mysteries of
your creation: Be friendly unto me: for I am the servant of the
same your God: the true worshipper of the Highest.

The Second Key
Invokes the Line of Spirit in the Tablet of Union EHNB
General Enochian Amplifier

ROMAN CHARACTERS:

Adgt vpaah zongom faaip Sald viiv L sobam Ialprg Izazaz
piadph casarma abramg ta talho paracleda Q ta lorslq turbs ooge
Baltoh Giui chis lusd orri Od micalp chis bia ozongon Lap noan
trof cors tage oq manin Iaidon Torzu gohel ZACAR ca cnoqod
ZAMRAN micalzo od ozazm vrelp Lap zir Ioiad

PHONETIC:

AD-GET VUH-PAH-AH ZONG OM FAH-AH-EEP SALD VEE-EEV EL
SOBAM YAL-POORJ EE-ZA-ZAZ PEE-ADF KASARMA ABRAM-GUH TA
TALHO PARA-KLAY-DA KWUH TA LOR-SEL-KWAH TOORBS OH-OH-
GAY BALTOH GEE-OO-EE KIS LOOSDUH OR-REE OD MEE-KALP KEES
BEE-AH OH-ZONG-ON LAP NOAN TROF KORS TAH-JEH OH-KWAH
MANIN YAH-EE-DON TOR-ZOO GO-HEL ZAKAR KAH KUH-NO-KWOD
ZAMRAN MEE-KAL-ZO OD OH-ZAZ-MUH VRELP LAP ZEER EE-YO-EE-
AD

ENGLISH TRANSLATION:

Can the Wings of the Winds understand your voices of Wonder?
O you the second of the first, whom the burning flames have
framed in the depth of my Jaws, whom I have prepared as cups
for a wedding or as the flowers in their beauty for the chamber
of Righteousness. Stronger are your feet than the barren stone:
and mightier are your voices than the manifold winds! For you
are become a building such as is not but in the mind of the All-
Powerful. Arise, saith the First, Move therefore unto his servants: Shew yourselves in power: and make me a strong Seething:
for I am of Him that liveth forever.

The Third Key
Invokes the Tablet of Air, angle Air of Air, and EXARP
(Use first in invocations of the Watchtower of the East)

ROMAN CHARACTERS:

Micma goho Piad zir comselh azien biab Os Londoh Norz Chis
othil Gigipah vndl chis ta puim Q mospleh teloch Quiin toltorg
chis ichisge m ozien ds brgda od torzul ili eol balzarg od aala
Thiln Os netaab dluga vomsarg lonsa capmiali vors cla homil
cocasb fafen izizop od miinoag de gnetaab vaun nanaeel panpir
Malpirgi caosg Pild noan unalah balt od vooan dooiap MAD
Goholor gohus amiran Micma Iehusoz cacacom od dooain noar
micaolz aaiom Casarmg gohia ZACAR uniglag od Imuamar
pugo plapli ananael Qaan

PHONETIC:

MIK-MA GOHO PEE-AD ZEER KOM-SAYL-HEH A-ZEE-EN BEE-AB OS
LON-DOH NORZ KEES OH-THEEL JEEH-JEEH-PAH VIH-NDL KEES TA-
POO-EEM KWUH MOS-PLAY TELOTCH KWEE-EEN TOLTORJ KEES EE-
KEES-JEH EM O-ZEE-EN DES BURJDA OD TORZOOL EELEE AY-OL
BALZARJ OD AH-AL-AH THEELN OS NE-TA-AB DUH-LOO-GAH
VOMSARJ LONSA KAP-MEE-AH-LEE VORS KLA HOMEEL KO-KAS-BUH
FAFEN EE-ZEE-ZOP OD MEE-EE-NO-AG DAY GUH-NEH-TAH-AB VA-
OON NA-NA-AY-EL PANPEER MALPEERGEE KAH-OS-GUH PEELD NO-
AN OO-NAL-AH BALT OD VOH-OH-AN DOH-OH-EE-AP MAD GOHO-
LOR GO-HOOS AH-MEEH-RAN MEEK-MA YAY-HOO-SOZ KAKAKOM
OD DO-OH-AH-EEN NO-AR MEE-KAH-OLZ AH-AH-EE-OM KA-SARM-
JUH GO-HEE-AH ZOD-A-KAR OO-NEEG-LAG OD EEM-OO-WAH-MAR
POO-GO PLAH-PLEE AH-NAH-NAH-EL KWAH-AH-AN

ENGLISH TRANSLATION:

Behold saith your God, I am a circle on whose hands stand
Twelve Kingdoms. Six are the seats of living breath, the rest are
as sharp sickles: or the horns of death wherein the Creatures of
the earth are to are not, except mine own hand, which sleep and
shall rise. In the first I made you stewards and placed you in
twelve seats of government, giving unto every one of you power
successively over 456, the true ages of time, to the intent that,
from your highest vessels and the corners of your governments,
you might work my power: pouring down the fires of life and
increase continually on the earth. Thus you are become the skirts
of Justice and Truth. In the name of the same your God lift up, I
say, yourselves. Behold his mercies flourish and Name is become
mighty amongst us. In whom we say Move, Descend and apply
yourselves unto us as unto the partakers of the secret wisdom of
your Creation.

The Fourth Key

Invokes the Tablet of Water, angle Water of Water, HCOMA
(Use first in invocations of the Watchtower of the West)

ROMAN CHARACTERS:

Othil lasdi babage od dorpha Gohol Gchisge avavago cormp pd dsonf vivdiv Casarmi oali Mapm Sobam ag cormpo crpl Casarmg croodzi chis od vgeg dst capimali chis capimaon Lonshin chis ta lo Cla Torgu Nor quasahi od F caosga Bagle zirenaiad Dsi od Apila Dooaip Qaal ZACAR od ZAMRAN Obelisong restel aaf Normolap

PHONETIC:

O-THEEL LAS-DEE BA-BA-JEH OD DOR-FA GOHOL GUH-KIS-JEH AVAVAGO KORMP PAY-DAY DUH-SON-FUH VEE-VUH-DEE-VUH KASARMEE OH-AH-LEE MAP-EM SOBAM AG KORMPO KUR-PUL KA-SARM-JUH KRO-OD-ZEE KEES OD VUH-GEJ DEST KA-PEE-MA-LEE KEES KA-PEE-MA-ON OD LON-SHIN KEES TA LO KLA TORGOO NOR KWAH-SAH-HEE OD EF KAH-OS-GAH BAH-GLAY ZEE-RAY-NYE-AD DES-EE OD AH-PEE-LA DO-OH-AH-EEP KWAH-AL ZAKAR OD ZAMRAN OH-BEL-EE-SONG REST-EL AH-AF NORMOLAP

ENGLISH TRANSLATION:

I have set my feet in the South, and have looked about me, saying, are not the thunders of increase numbered 33, which reign in the second Angle, under whom I have placed 9639 whom none hath yet numbered, but one, in whom the Second beginning of things are and wax strong which also successively are the numbers of time: and their powers are as the first 456: Arise, you sons of pleasure, and visit the earth: for I am the Lord your God, which is and liveth. In the name of the Creator Move and shew yourselves as pleasant deliverers that you may praise him among the sons of men.

The Fifth Key

Invokes the tablet of Earth, angle of Earth of Earth, NANTA
(Use first in invocations of the Watchtower of the North)

ROMAN CHARACTERS:

Sapah zimii duiv od noas ta qaanis adroch dorphal Caosg od faonts peripsol tablior Casarm amipzi nazarth af od dlugar zizop zlida caosgi toltorgi od zchis esiasch L taviu od iaod thild ds peral hubar Peoal soba cormfa chis ta la uls od Qcocasb Ca niis od Darbs Qaas Fetharzi od bliora iaial ednas cicles Bagle Geiad iL

PHONETIC:

SA-PAH ZEE-MEE-EE DOO-EEV OD NO-AS TAH-KWAH-NIS AD-ROTCH DOR-FAL KA-OS-JUH OD FA-ONTS PEE-REEP-SOL TA-BLEE-OR KASARM AH-MEEP-ZEE NA-ZARTH AF OD DUH-LOO-GAR ZEE-ZOP ZOD-LEE-DAH KA-OS-JEE TOL-TOR-JEE OD ZOD-KEES AY-SEE-AK EL TA-WEE-OO OD EE-AH-OD THEELD DES PAY-RAL HOO-BAR PAY-OH-AL SOBA KORMFA KEES TA LA YULZ OD KWUH-KO-KAS-BUH SA NEE-EES OD DARBZ KWAH-AS FETH-AR-ZEE OD BLEE-OH-RAH EE-YA-EE-AL EDNAS KEE-KLAYZ BA-GLAY GAY-EE-YAD EEL

ENGLISH TRANSLATION:

The mighty sounds have entered into the third angle, and are become as olives in the olive mount looking with gladness upon the earth and dwelling in the brightness of the heavens as continual comforters, unto whom I fastened 19 Pillars of gladness, and gave them vessels to water the earth with her creatures, and they are the brothers of the first and second and the beginning of their own seats which are garnished with 69,636 continually burning lamps whose numbers are as the first the ends and the contents of time. Therefore come you and obey your creation, visit us in peace and comfort conclude us as receivers of your mysteries: for why? Our Lord and Master is all one.

The Sixth Key
Invokes the tablet of Fire, angle Fire of Fire, BITOM
(Use first in invocations of the Watchtower of the South)

ROMAN CHARACTERS:

Gah s diu chis em micalzo pilzin sobam El harg mir babalon od obloc samvelg dlugar malprg arcaosgi od Acam canal sobolzar fbliard caosgi od chis anetab od miam ta viv od d Darsar solpeth bien Brita od zacam gmicalzo sobhaath trian Luiahe odecrin MAD Qaaon

PHONETIC:

GAH ES DEE-OO KEES EM MEE-KAL-ZO PEEL-ZEEN SOBAM EL HARJ MEER BABALON OD OB-LOK SAM-VELJ DUH-LOO-GAR MAL-POORJ AR-KA-OS-JEE OD AKAM SANAL SOBOLZAR EF-BLEE-ARD KA-OS-JEE OD KEES AH-NAY-TAB OD MEE-AM TA VEEV OD DUH DARSAR SOL-PETH BEE-EN BREE-TAH OD ZA-KAM GUH-MEE-KAL-ZO SOB-HA-ATH TREE-AN LOO-EE-AH-HAY OH-DEH-KREEN MAD KWUH-AH-AH-ON

ENGLISH TRANSLATION:

The Spirits of the fourth Angle are Nine, mighty in the firmament of waters, Whom the first hath planted a torment to the wicked and a garland to the righteous giving unto them fiery darts to vanne the earth and 7699 continual workmen whose courses visit with comfort the earth and are in government and continuance as the second and the third wherefore hearken unto my voice I have talked of you and I move you in power and presence, whose works shall be a song of honour, and the praise of your God in your Creation.

The Seventh Key
Invokes the angle Water of Air in the Watchtower of the East
(Use second for Water of Air)

ROMAN CHARACTERS:

Raas isalman paradiz oecrimi aao ialpirgah quiin enay butmon od inoas ni paradial casarmg vgear chirlan od zonac Luciftian cors ta vaul zirn tolhami Soba Londoh od miam chis tad o des vmadea od pibliar Othil rit od miam Cnoquol Rit ZACAR ZAMRAN oecrimi Qadah od omicaolz aaiom Bagle papnor idlugam lonshi od umplif vgegi Bigliad.

PHONETIC:

RAH-AS EE-SALMAN PA-RA-DEE-ZOD OH-AY-KREE-MEE AH-AH-OH EE-YAL-PEER-GAH KWEE-EEN EN-AH-EE BOOT-MON OD EEN-OH-AS NEE PA-RA-DEE-AL KA-SARM-JUH VUH-GAY-AR KEERLAN OD ZONAK LOO-KEEF-TEE-AN KORS TA VAH-OOL ZIRN TOL-HA-MEE SOBA LON-DOH OD MEE-AM KEES-TAD O DES VUH-MA-DAY-AH OD PEEB-LEE-AR OH-THEEL-REET OD MEE-AM KUH-NO-KOL REET ZAKAR ZAMRAN OH-AY-KREE-MEE KWUH-AH-DAH OD OH-MEE-KAH-OL-ZOD AH-AH-EE-OM BA-GLAY PAPNOR EED-LOO-GAM LON-SHEE OD OOM-PLEEF VUH-GAY-JEE BEEG-LEE-AD

ENGLISH TRANSLATION:

The East is a house of virgins singing praises amongst the flames of the first glory, wherein the Lord hath opened his mouth and they are become 28 Living dwellings in whom the strength of men rejoiceth and they are apparelled with ornaments of brightness such as work wonders on all creatures Whose kingdoms and continuance are as the Third and Fourth, strong towers and places of comfort, the Seats of Mercy and Continuance. O ye Servants of Mercy, Move! Appear! Sing praises unto the Creator; and be mighty amongst us. For that to this remembrance is given power, and our strength waxeth strong in our Comforter.

The Eighth Key
Invokes the angle Earth of Air in the Watchtower of the East
(Use second for Earth of Air)

ROMAN CHARACTERS:

Bazmelo I ta piripson oln Nazavabh ox casarmg vran Chis vgeg dsabramg baltoha goho iad solamian trian ta lolcis Abaiuonin od aziagier rior Irgil chis da ds paaox busd Caosgo ds chis od ipuran teloah cacarg O isalman loncho od Vovina carbaf Niiso Bagle avavago gohon Niiso bagle momao siaion od mabza Iadoiasmomar poilp Niis ZAMRAN ciaofi caosgo od bliors od corsi ta abramig

PHONETIC:

BAZ-MAY-LO EE-TA PEE-REEP-SON OLN NA-ZA-VABH OKS KA-SARM-JUH VUH-RAN KEES VUH-GEJ DUH-SA-BRAM-GUH BAL-TO-HA GO-HO-EE-AD SO-LA-MEE-AN TREE-AN TA-LOL-SEES A-BA-EE-WO-NEEN OD A-ZEE-AH-JEE-ER REE-OR EER-GIL KEES DA DUHS PA-AH-OKS BOOSD KA-OS-GO DES KIS O-DEE-POO-RAN TAY-LO-AH KA-KARJ O EE-SAL-MAN LON-KO OD VO-VEE-NA KAR-BAF NEE-EE-SO BA-GLAY AH-VA-VA-GO GO-HON NEE-EE-SO BA-GLAY MO-MA-OH SEE-AH-EE-ON OD MAB-ZA YAD-OH-EE-AS-MO-MAR PO-EELP NEE-EES ZAM-RAN KEE-AH-OH-FEE KA-OS-GO OD BLEE-ORS OD KOR-SEE TA A-BRA-MEEG

ENGLISH TRANSLATION:

The Midday the first is as the third heaven made of 26 Hyacinth Pillars in whom the Elders are become strong which I have pre-pared for mine own Righteousness sayeth the Lord whose long continuance shall be as bucklers to the Stooping Dragon and like unto the harvest of a Widow. How many are there which remain in the glory of the earth which are and shall not see death until this house fall and the Dragon sink. Come away, for the Thun-ders have spoken: Come away, for the Crowns of the Temple and the coat of Him that is, was, and shall be crowned are divided Come Appear to the terror of the earth and to our comfort and to our comfort and of such as are prepared.

The Ninth Key

Invokes the angle of Fire of Air in the Watchtower of the East
(Use second for Fire of Air)

ROMAN CHARACTERS:

Micaoli bransg prgel napta ialpor ds brin efafafe P vonpho olani od obza Sobca vpaah chis tatan od tranan balye alar lusda soboln od chis holq Cnoquodi cial vnal aldon mom caosgo ta las ollor gnay limlal Amma chiis Sobca madrid zchis ooanoan chis aviny drilpi caosgin od butmoni parm zumvi Cnila Daziz ethamz achildao od mirc ozol chis pidiai Collal Ulcinin asobam ucim Bagle Iadbaltoh chirlan par Niiso od ip ofafafe Bagle acosasb icorsca unig blior

PHONETIC:

MEE-KA-OH-LEE BRANS-GUH POOR-GEL NAP-TA YAL-POR DES-BREEN AY-FAH-FAH-FAY PUH VON-FO OH-LA-NEE OD OB-ZA SOB-KA VUH-PAH-AH KEES TA-TAN OD TRA-NAN BA-LEE-AY A-LAR LOOS-DA SO-BOLN OD KEES-HOL-KWAH KUH-NO-KWO-DEE SEE-AL VUH-NAL AL-DON MOM KA-OS-GO TA LAS-OL-LOR GUH-NAY LEEM-LAL AM-MA KEE-EES SOB-KA MA-DREED ZOD-KEES OH-OH-AH-NO-AN KEES AH-VEE-NEE DRIL-PEE KA-OS-JEEN OD BOOT-MO-NEE PARM ZOOM-VEE KUH-NEE-LA DAZ-EES AY-THAM-ZOD AH-KEEL-DA-OH OD MEERK OH-ZOL KIS PEE-DEE-AH-EE KOL-LAL OOL-SEE-NEEN A-SO-BAM OO-SEEM BA-GLAY EE-YAD-BAL-TOH KIR-LAN PAR NEE-EE-SO OD EEP OH-FA-FA-FAY BA-GLAY AH-KO-KASB EE-KORS-KA VUH-NIG BLEE-OR

ENGLISH TRANSLATION:

A mighty guard of fire with two-edged swords flaming (which have eight Vials of wrath for two times and a half: whose wings are of wormwood and of the marrow of salt,) have settled their feet in the West, and are measured with their 9996 ministers. These gather up the moss of the earth as the rich man doth his treasure: Cursed are they whose iniquities they are in their eyes are mill-stones greater than the earth and from their mouths run seas of blood: Their heads are covered with diamond: and upon their heads are marble sleeves. Happy is he, on whom they frown not. For why? The God of Righteousness rejoiceth in them. Come away and not your Viols for the time is such as requireth Comfort.

The Tenth Key
Invokes the angle Air of Water in the Watchtower of the West
(Use second for Air of Water)

ROMAN CHARACTERS:

Coraxo chis cormp od blans Lucal aziazor paeb soba lilonon chis virq op eophan od raclir maasi bagle caosgi ds ialpon dosig od basgim od oxex dazis siatris od salbrox cynxir faboan Unalchis Const ds daox cocasg ol oanio yor vohim ol gizyax od eors cocasg plosi molui ds pageip larag om droln matorb cocasb emna L patralx yolci matb nomig monons olora gnay angelard Ohio ohio ohio ohio ohio ohio noib ohio caosgon Bagle madrid i zirop chiso drilpa Niiso crip ip nidali

PHONETIC:

KO-RAK-SO KEES KORMP OD BLANZ LOO-KAL AH-ZEE-AH-ZOR PA-EB SO-BA LEE-LO-NON KEES OP VEER-KWUH AY-OH-FAN OD RA-KLEER MA-AH-SEE BA-GLAY KA-OS-JEE DES YAL-PON DO-SEEG OD BAS-GEEM OD OKS-AYKS DAH-ZEES SEE-AH-TREES OD SAL-BROKS SINKS-EER FA-BO-AN YOON-AL-KIS KONST DES DA-OKS KO-KAS-JUH OL OH-AH-NEE-OH YOR VO-HEEM OL GIZ-EE-AKS OD AY-ORZ KO-KAS-JUH PLO-SEE MOL-WEE DES PA-GAY-EEP LA-RAG OM DROL-NUH MA-TORB KO-KAS-BUH EM-NA EL PA-TRALKS YOL-SEE MAH-TUB NO-MEEG MO-NONS OH-LO-RA GUH-NAY AN-GAY-LARD O-HEE-O O-HEE-O O-HEE-O O-HEE-O O-HEE-O O-HEE-O NO-EEB O-HEE-O KA-OS-GON BA-GLAY MA-DREED EE ZEE-ROP KEE-SO DREEL-PA NEE-EE-SO KREEP EEP NEE-DA-LEE

ENGLISH TRANSLATION:

The Thunders of Judgment and Wrath are numbered and are harbored in the North in the likeness of an Oak whose branches are 22 nests of lamentation and weeping laid up for the earth which burn night and day: and vomit out the heads of scorpions and live sulphur mingled with poison These be the thunders that 5678 times in the twenty-fourth part of a moment roar with a hundred mighty earthquakes and a thousand times as many surges which rest not neither know any time here. One rock bringeth forth a thousand, even as the heart of man doth his thoughts Woe! Woe! Woe! Woe! Woe! Woe! Yea, Woe be to the earth for her iniquity is, was, and shall be great. Come away but not your noises.

The Eleventh Key
Invokes the angle Earth of Water in the Watchtower of the West
(Use second for Earth of Water)

ROMAN CHARACTERS:

Oxiayal holdo od zirom O Coraxo ds zildar raasy od vabzir camliax od bahal Niiso salman teloch Casarman holq od ti ta zchis soba cormf i ga Niisa Bagle abramg noncp ZACARe ca od ZAMRAN odo cicle qaa Zorge lap zirdo noco Mad Hoath Iaida

PHONETIC:

OKS-EE-AH-AL HOL-DO OD ZEER-OM OH KO-RAKS-OH DES ZEEL-DAR RA-AH-SEE OD VAB-ZEER KAM-LEE-AKS OD BA-HAL NEE-EE-SO SAL-MAN TAY-LOTCH KA-SAR-MAN HOL-KWAH OD TEE TAH ZOD-KEES SO-BA KORMF EE GAH NEE-EE-SA BA-GLAY AH-BRAM-GUH NON-SPUH ZAKAR-AY KA OD ZAMRAN ODO KEE-KLAY KWUH-AH-AH ZORJ LAP ZEER-DO NOKO MAD HO-ATH EE-YA-EE-DAH

ENGLISH TRANSLATION:

The mighty seat groaned and there were five thunders which flew into the East and the Eagle spake and cried with a loud voice Come away and they gathered them together in the house of death of whom it is measured and it is as they are whose number is 31. Come away For I have prepared for you Move therefore and shew yourselves open the mysteries of your Creation Be friendly unto me for I am the servant of the same your God the true worshipper of the Highest.

The Twelfth Key
Invokes the angle of Fire of Water in the Watchtower of the West
(Use second for Fire of Water)

ROMAN CHARACTERS:

Nonci dsonf Babage od chis ob hubaio tibibp allar atraah od ef drix fafen Mian ar Enay ovof soba dooain aai i VONPH ZACAR gohus od ZAMRAM odo cicle Qaa Zorge lap zirdo noco MAD Hoath Iaida

PHONETIC:

NON-SEE DUH-SON-FUH BA-BA-JEH OD KEES OB HOO-BA-EE-OH TEE-BEEB-PUH, AL-LAR A-TRA-AH OD EF DREEKS FA-FEN MEE-AN AR EN-AY OH-VOF SO-BA DO-OH-AH-EEN AH-AH-EE EE VONF ZAKAR GO-HOOS OD ZAMRAN ODO KEE-KLAY KWUH-AH-AH ZORJ LAP ZEER-DO NOKO MAD HO-ATH EE-YA-EE-DAH

ENGLISH TRANSLATION:

O you that reign in the south and are the 28 lanterns of sorrow bind up your girdles and visit us bring down your train 3663 that the Lord may be magnified whose name amongst you is Wrath Move, I say, and shew yourselves open the mysteries of your Creation Be friendly unto me for I am the servant of the same your God the true worshipper of the Highest.

The Thirteenth Key
Invokes the angle Air of Earth in the Watchtower of the North
(Use second for Air of Earth)

ROMAN CHARACTERS:

Napeai Babagen ds brin ux ooaona lring vonph doalim eolis
ollog orsba ds chis affa Micma isro MAD od Lonshitox ds iumd
aai GROSB ZACAR od ZAMRAN odo cicle Qaa zorge lap zirdo
noco MAD Hoath Iaida

PHONETIC:

NA-PAY-AH-EE BA-BA-JEN DES BREEN YOOKS OH-OH-AH-NA EL-
REENG VONF DO-AH-LEEM AY-OH-LEES OL-LOG ORZ-BA DES KEES
AF-FA MEEK-MA EES-RO MAD OD LON-SHEE-TOKS DES JUH-OOMD
AH-AH-EE GROS-BUH ZAKAR OD ZAMRAN ODO KEE-KLAY KWUH-
AH-AH ZORJ LAP ZEER-DO NOKO MAD HO-ATH EE-YA-EE-DAH

ENGLISH TRANSLATION:

O you swords of the south which have 42 eyes to stir up the
wrath of sin making men drunken which are empty: Behold the
promise of God and his power which is called amongst you a
bitter sting: Move and shew yourselves open the mysteries of
your Creation Be friendly unto me for I am the servant of the
same your God the true worshipper of the Highest.

The Fourteenth Key
Invokes the angle Water of Earth in the Watchtower of the North
(Use second for Water of Earth)

ROMAN CHARACTERS:

Noromi bagie pasbs oiad ds trint mirc ol thil dods tolham caosgo
Homin ds brin oroch Quar Micma bial oiad aisro tox dsivm aai
Baltim ZACAR od ZAMRAN odo cicle Qaa zorge lap zirdo noco
MAD hoath Iaida

PHONETIC:

NO-RO-MEE BA-JEE-AY PAS-BIZ OH-EE-AD DES TREEN-TUH MEER-
KUH OL THEEL DODS TOL-HAM KA-OS-GO HO-MEEN DES BREEN
OROK KOO-AR MEEK-MA BEE-AL OH-EE-AD AH-EES-RO TOKS DES-

YOOM AH-AH-EE BAL-TEEM ZAKAR OD ZAMRAN ODO KEE-KLAY KWUH-AH-AH ZORJ LAP ZEER-DO NOKO MAD HO-ATH EE-YA-EE-DAH

ENGLISH TRANSLATION:

O you sons of fury the daughters of the Just which sit upon 24 seats vexing all creatures of the Earth with age which have 1636 under you Behold the voice of God the promise of him which is called amongst you Fury or Extreme Justice- Move and shew yourselves open the mysteries of your Creation Be friendly unto me for I am the servant of the same your God the true worshipper of the Highest.

The Fifteenth Key
Invokes the angle Fire of Earth in the Watchtower of the North
(Use second for Fire of Earth)

ROMAN CHARACTERS:

Ils tabaan lialprt casarman upaahi chis darg dsoado caosgi orscor ds omax monasci Baeouib od emetgis iaiadix ZACAR od ZAMRAN odo cicle Qaa zorge lap zirdo Noco MAD hoath Iaida

PHONETIC:

YEELS TA-BA-AN LEE-AL-PURT KASARMAN OO-PA-AH-HEE KEES DARJUH DES OH-AH-DO KA-OS-JEE ORS-KOR DES OH-MAKS MO-NAS-KEE BYAY-OH-OO-EEB OD AY-MET-JEES EE-YAH-EE-AH-DEEKS ZAKAR OD ZAMRAN ODO KEE-KLAY KWUH-AH-AH ZORJ LAP ZEER-DO NOKO MAD HO-ATH EE-YA-EE-DAH

ENGLISH TRANSLATION:

O thou the governor of the first flame under whose wings are 6739 which weave the Earth with dryness which knowest of the Great Name Righteousness and the seal of Honour- Move and shew yourselves open the mysteries of your Creation Be friendly unto me for I am the servant of the same your God the true worshipper of the Highest.

The Sixteenth Key
Invokes the angle Air of Fire in the watchtower of the South
(Use second for Air of Fire)

ROMAN CHARACTERS:

Ils vivialprt salman balt ds acroodzi busd od bliorax balit dsinsi caosg lusdan Emod dsom od tliob drilpa geh yls Madzilodarp ZACAR od ZAMRAN odo cicle Qaa zorge lap zirdo noco MAD hoath Iaida

PHONETIC:

YEELS VEEV-YAL-PURT SAL-MAN BALT DES BREEN A-KROH-OD-ZEE BOOSD OD BLEE-OH-RAKS BALEET DES-EEN-SEE KA-OS-JUH LOOS-DAN AY-MOD DUH-SOM OD TUH-LEE-OB DREEL-PA JEH YEELS MAD-ZEE-LO-DARP ZAKAR OD ZAMRAN ODO KEE-KLAY KWUH-AH-AH ZORJ LAP ZEER-DO NOKO MAD HO-ATH EE-YA-EE-DAH

ENGLISH TRANSLATION:

O thou second flame the house of Justice which hast thy beginning in glory: and shalt comfort the Just: which walkest on the Earth with 8763 feet which understand and separate creatures: Great art thou in the God of stretch-forth-and-conquer. Move and shew yourselves open the mysteries of your Creation Be friendly unto me for I am the servant of the same your God the true worshipper of the Highest.

The Seventeenth Key
Invokes the angle Water of Fire in the Watchtower of the South
(Use second for Water of Fire)

ROMAN CHARACTERS:

Ils dialprt soba upaah chis nanba zixlay dodsih od brint Faxs hubaro tustax ylsi sobaiad I vonpounph Aldon daxil od tatar ZACAR od ZAMRAN odo cicle Qaa zorge lap zirdo Noco MAD hoath Iaida

PHONETIC:

YEELS DEE-AL PERT SO-BA VUH-PA-AH KEES NAN-BA ZEEKS-LA-EE DOD-SEEH OD BREENT FAKS-UHZ HOO-BA-RO TAS-TAKS YEEL-SEE SO-BA-EE-AD EE VON-PO-OONF AL-DON DAKS-EEL OD TO-A-TAR ZAKAR OD ZAMRAN ODO KEE-KLAY KWUH-AH-AH ZORJ LAP ZEER-DO NOKO MAD HO-ATH EE-YA-EE-DAH

ENGLISH TRANSLATION:

O thou third flame whose wings are thorns to stir up vexation: and hast 7336 living lamps going before thee whose God is Wrath in Anger- Gird up thy loins and hearken Move and shew yourselves open the mysteries of your Creation Be friendly unto me for I am the servant of the same your God the true worshipper of the Highest.

The Eighteenth Key
Invokes the angle Earth of Fire in the Watchtower of the South
(Use second for Earth of Fire)

ROMAN CHARACTERS:

Ils Micaolz olpirt ialprg Bliors ds odo Busdir oiad ovoars caosgo Casarmg Laiad eran brints casasam ds iumd aqlo adohi MOZ od maoffas Bolp comobliort pambt ZACAR od ZAMRAN odo cicle Qaa zorge lap zirdo Noco MAD hoath Iaida

PHONETIC:

YEELS MEE-KA-OL-ZOD OL-PEERT YAL-POORJ BLEE-ORS DES ODO BOOS-DEER OH-EE-AD OH-VO-ARZ KA-OS-GO KA-SARM-JUH LA-EE-AD AY-RAN BREENTS KA-SA-SAM DES EE-YOOMD AH-KWUH-LO A-

DO-HEE MOZ OD MA-OF-FAS BOLP KO-MO-BLEE-ORT PAM-BUT ZAKAR AY KA OD ZAMRAN ODO KEE-KLAY KWUH-AH-AH ZORJ LAP ZEER-DO NOKO MAD HO-ATH EE-YA-EE-DAH

ENGLISH TRANSLATION:

O thou mighty light and burning flame of comfort which open-est the glory of God to the center of the earth In whom the 6332 secrets of truth have their abiding which is called in thy kingdom Joy and not to be measured- Be thou a window of comfort unto me. Move and shew yourselves open the mysteries of your Creation Be friendly unto me for I am the servant of the same your God the true worshipper of the Highest.

The Key of the Thirty Aethyrs
Invokes All Thirty Aethyrs

ROMAN CHARACTERS:

Madriax ds praf (Name of Aethyr) chis Micaolz saanir caosgo od fisis balzizras Iaida nonca gohulim Micma adoian MAD Iaod Bliorb sabaooaona chis Luciftias peripsol ds abraassa noncf netaaib caosgi od tilb adphaht damploz tooat noncf gmicalzoma Lrasd tofglo marb yarry IDOIGO od torzulp iaodaf gohol caosga tabaord saanir od christeos yrpoil tiobl Busdir tilb noaln paid orsba od dodrmni zylna Elzaptilb parmgi peripsax od ta qurlst booapis Lnibm ovcho symp od Christeos Agtoltorn mirc q tiobl Lel Ton paombd dilzmo aspian Od christeos Ag L tortorn parach asymp Cordziz dodpal od fifalz Lsmnad od fargt bams omaoas Conisbra od auavox tonug Orscatbl noasmi tabges Levithmong unchi omptilb ors Bagle Moooah olcordziz L capimao ixomaxip od cacocasb gosaa Baglen pii tianta ababalond od faorgt telocvovim Madriiax torzu oadriax orocha aboapri Tabaori priaz artabas Adrpan corsta dobix Yolcam priazi ar coazior Od quasb qting Ripir paaoxt sagacor uml od prdzar cacrg Aoiveae cormpt TORZU ZACAR od ZAMRAN aspt sibsi butmona ds surzas tia baltan Odo cicle Qaa Od Ozama plapli Iadnamad

PHONETIC:

MAD-REE-AKS DES PRAF (Name Of Aethyr) KEES MEE-KA-OLZ SA-AH-NEER KA-OS-GO OD FEE-SEES BAL-ZEEZ-RAS EE-YA-EE-DAH NONSA GO-HOO-LEEM MEEK-MA A-DO-EE-AN MAD EE-AH-OD BLEE-ORB SA-BA-OH-OH-AH-OH-NA KEES LOO-KEEF-TEE-AS PAY-REEP-SOL DES A-BRA-AS-SA NON-SUF NE-TAH-AH-EEB KA-OS-JEE OD TEELB AD-FA-TUH DAM-PLOZ TO-OH-AT NON-SUF GUH-MEE-KAL-ZO-MA EL-RAS-DUH TOF-GLO MARB YAR-REE EE-DO-EE-GO OD TOR-ZOOLP YA-OH-DAF GO-HOL KA-OS-GA TA-BA-ORD SA-AH-NEER OD KREES-TAY-OS EER-PO-EEL TEE-OH-BUL BOOS-DEER TEEL-BUH NO-AL-NUH PA-EED ORS-BA OD DOD-RUM-NEE ZEELNA EL-ZAP-TEELB PARM-GEE PAY-REEP-SAKS OD TA KOORLST BO-OH-AH-PEES EL-NEEB-UM OH-VUH-KO SIMP OD KREES-TAY-OS AG-TOL-TORN MEERK KWAH TEE-OH-BEL LEL TON PA-OM-DUH DEELZ-MO AS-PEE-AN OD KREES-TAY-OS AG-UL-TER-TORN PA-RACH A-SEEMP KORD-ZEEZ DOD-PAL OD FEE-FALZ ULZ-MUH-NAD OD FAR-JET BAMZ OH-MA-OH-AS KO-NEES-BRA OD AH-WAH-VOKS TO-NUJ ORZ-CAT-BUL NO-AS-MEE TAB-JESS LAY-VEETH-MONG OON-KEE OM-PUH-TEELB ORZ BA-GLAY MO-OH-OH-AH OL-CORD-ZEEZ EL-KA-PEE-MA-OH EEKS-OH-MAKS-EEP OD KA-KO-KAS-BUH GO-SA-AH BA-GLEN PEE-EE TEE-AN-TA A-BA-BA-LON-DUH OD FA-OR-JET TAY-LOTCH-VO-VEEM MA-DREE-EE-YAKS TOR-ZOO OH-AH-DREE-AKS OH-RO-KA AH-BO-AH-PREE TA-BA-OH-REE PREE-AZ AR-TA-BAS AH-DIR-PAN KOR-STA DO-BEEKS YOL-KAM PREE-AH-ZEE AR-KO-AH-ZEE-OR OD KWAS-BUH KWAH-TINJ REE-PEER PA-AH-OKS-TUH SA-GA-KOR VUM-UL OD PURD-ZAR KA-KURJ AH-OO-EE-VAY-AH-AY KORM-PUT-TUH TOR-ZOO ZAKAR OD ZAMRAN AS-PUT SEEB-SEE BOOT-MO-NA DES SOOR-ZAS TEE-AH BAL-TAN ODO KEE-KLAY KWAH-AH-AH OD OH-ZAZ-MA PLA-PLEE EE-YAD-NA-MAD

ENGLISH TRANSLATION:

O you Heavens which dwell in (Name of Aethyr), are mighty in the parts of the earth, and execute the Judgment of the highest to you it is said, Behold the Face of your God, the beginning of Comfort: whose eyes are the brightness of the heavens: which provided you for the Government of the Earth, and her unspeakable variety, furnishing you with a power of understanding to dispose all things according to the Providence of Him that sitteth on the holy Throne and rose up in the beginning saying, The Earth Let her be governed by her parts and let there be Division in her, that the glory of her may be always drunken and vexed in itself: Her course, let it run with the Heavens: and as a handmaid let her serve them: One season, let it confound another, and let there be no Creature upon or within her the same: All her members, let them differ in their qualities, and let there be no one Creature equal with another The reasonable Creatures of the Earth or Men let them vex and weed out one another: and the dwelling places, let them forget their Names: The work of man and his pomp, let them be defaced: His buildings let them become Caves for the beasts of the field: Confound her understanding with darkness. For why? It repenteth me I made Man. One while let her be known, and another while a stranger: because she is the bed of an Harlot, and the dwelling place of him that is fallen. O you heavens arise, the lower heavens underneath you, let them serve you: Govern those that govern: Cast down such as fall: Bring forth with those that increase: And destroy the rotten: No place let it remain in one number: Add and diminish until the stars be numbered: Arise, Move, and Appear before The Covenant of his mouth, which he hath sworn unto us in his justice. Open the Mysteries of your Creation, and make us partakers of undefiled knowledge.

Appendix B
Areas of Ambiguity for Exploration and Experimentation

There are several areas within the instructions the angels gave to Dee and Kelly that are either quite vague and capable of multiple interpretations. There are other cases where the Golden Dawn adepts just simply chose to do something quite different from the original instructions. The following are some alternate ways of approaching work with the watchtowers that you may find useful.

Other Letter Combinations

As I said in the chapter on the hierarchy of the watchtowers, there are other ways of calculating the names of some of these angels. The method that is most commonly used outside of the Golden Dawn is to take the letter directly from the horizontally adjacent square of the black cross in forming the five-lettered names of the archangels, "super" lesser angels and the names of the kakodaimons. The other popular Golden Dawn method assigns the letters from the Tablet of Union to each of the subangles, so that the names of lesser angels from that subangle share the same letter. The interesting result of this method is that it basically makes the letters of the Tablet of Union into mini versions of the Tablets. The only problem with this method is that it does not match the instructions of the angels. This area is certainly worthy of some more practical experimentation. In my experience, every way brings an angelic communication.

PRACTICAL ENOCHIAN MAGICK

This brings up an interesting possibility. It seems that virtually any combination of letters from any of the tablets produce an intelligence. You could try invoking angels formed from vertical columns, or combine letters from multiple angels to produce the exact being you wish to commune with. Feel free to be creative in this matter and record your results.

Scrying the Pyramid Squares

The most popular Golden Dawn Enochian practice was simply to imagine the pyramid square of a letter of the tablets as a gateway, and to explore the astral world behind that gateway. Personally, I have found invoking the angels directly more fruitful, but exploring the watchtowers in this way can quite easily be conducted as a simple variation on the "Tarot Archetype Pathworking" in the Practitioner level of the New Hermetics.

In short, there are a nearly infinite number of angelic personages described in this magical system that have never been satisfactorily explored. Names of angels appear in the tablets of the bonorum horizontally in each line. Vertical lines might invoke more. Every combination of letters from the various tablets of Dee and Kelly's scrying sessions seems to yield the name of an angelic personage. How deeply you want to go into this is up to you.

The angels from the Sigillum Dei Aemeth are also quite easy to contact. These are largely the angels that delivered this system in the first place, and it is rather odd that so few have explored these beings. We will discuss them a bit more in the next appendix.

Further, the guiding voices behind this work were quite often the four archangels Raphael, Uriel, Gabriel and Michael, as well as a few others not represented in the various tablets. These beings may yet have further insights into this system for you. All you have to do is ask.

Appendix C
Brief Analysis of the Sigillum Dei Aemeth

This icon is a truly fascinating piece of magical imagery that is made even more fascinating when it is considered that it was delivered to Dee and Kelly slowly, piece by piece, in a vision in the shewstone. The story of its reception is quite amazing too.

The angels told Dee that the proper seal for their work could be found in books he already possessed. So Dee diligently went through his library of rare occult books, and found two different versions of a sacred seal in *The Sworn Book of Honorius (Liber Juratus)* and *Oedipus Aegypticus*. But the two seals were different in many respects. So Dee and Kelly consulted the angels on which one was correct. The angel Michael instructed them that both versions were corrupt and slowly revealed a new symbol that bears only superficial resemblance to those found in the other books.

In describing this symbol, I will begin at the outer edge and move inward. The outermost circle contains forty sections containing letters and numbers in combination. These symbols, as were many of the symbols revealed to Dee and Kelly, were slowly brought before Kelly's eyes in the shewstone by angelic figures who had the symbols on their chests.

The numbers add up to 440, adding one to this we get 441, the enumeration of the Hebrew word אמת or "Aemeth," which signifies "Truth." Seven of the letters arouond the circumference are capitalized. These capital letters begin the names of special hidden angels within the system. The numbers indicate how many spaces you have to count to get to the next letter of the beings name. When the number is above the letter you count clockwise, and when below counter-clockwise. The name is completed when you get to a letter that doesn't have a number.

Through this process these seven names are revealed:

Galas (Moon)
Gethog (Saturn)
Thaoth (Mercury)
Horlωn (Jupiter)
Innon (Mars)
Aaoth (Sun)
Galethog (Venus)

In conducting this process you will find that two of the names actually end up with two a's, Thaaoth and Galaas, but Dee and Kelly were instructed to delete these double letters. The planetary associations I give are based on the Heptarchia, and may or not be correct. These beings are apparently of great power. Each of these beings has a sigil, and these are placed in the seven semicircles that are just inside the outermost circle.

Moving inward, we come to a heptagon filled with letters. These letters can be turned into a grid like this:

Z	l	l	R	H	i	a
a	Z	G	a	a	c	b
p	a	u	p	n	h	r
h	d	m	h	i	a	i
k	k	a	a	e	e	e
i	i	e	e	l	l	l
e	e	l	l	M	G	✠

Reading the columns downward starting at the upper left we discover the names of the seven planetary archangels Zaphkiel, Zadkiel, Camael, Raphael, Haniel, Michael, Gabriel.

Directly within this outer heptagon there are a set of letters and numbers. These too can be placed into a seven by seven grid.

S	A	A	I²¹⸝₈	E	M	E⁸
B	T	Z	K	A	S	E³⁰
H	E	I	D	E	N	E
D	E	I	M	O	³⁰	A
I²⁶	M	E	G	C	B	E
I	L	A	O	I²¹⸝₈	V	N
I	H	R	L	A	A	²¹⸝₈

Reading this grid in a zig-zag pattern you can find the names of more angels relating to the seven planets. Keeping in mind that the number ciphers are equivalent to "l" or "el" where they occur, we find the names, Sabathiel, Zedekiel, Madimiel, Semeliel, Nogahel, Corabiel, Levanael.

Moving inward, we come to four sets of seven names wrapping around within the heptagram and heptagons. These names can be found in the above grid, although a simplified version will make them easier to find. There names can be read diagonally from the corners of the grid. Much of the Enochian material was delivered by these beings directly. The Sons of Light and their Sons also rule over the Heptarchia Mystica.

S	A	A	I	E	M	E
B	T	Z	K	A	S	E
H	E	I	D	E	N	E
D	E	I	M	O	L	A
I	M	E	G	C	B	E
I	L	A	O	I	V	N
I	H	R	L	A	A	E

These are the Daughters of Light:

E
Me
Ese
Iana
Akele
Azdobn
Stimcul

The Sons of Light:

I
Ih
Ilr
Dmal
Heeoa
Beigia
Stimcul

The Daughters of the Daughters of Light:

S
Ab
Ath
Ized
Ekiei
Madimi
Esemeli

The Sons of the Sons of Light:

L (El)
Aw
Ave

Liba
Rocle
Hagone(l)
Ilemese

Then within and around the small central pentagram we find the names of the planetary angels once again.

On the back of the Sigillum dei Aemeth is this symbol:

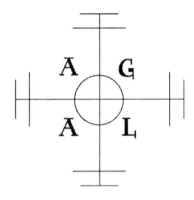

Appendix D
Brief Analysis of the Holy Table and Lamen

Both the Holy Table and the lamen are based on the following diagram, which contains the names of the kings and princes of the Heptarchia backward with their initial letter 'b' removed.

o	g	o	n	r	o	l	e	g	o	b	o
s	e	f	a	f	e	l	e	l	a	b	a
o	n	o	m	t	u	r	o	p	e	n	y
n	o	d	s	i	l	l	o	p	s	a	n
s	e	g	r	o	r	n	e	s	p	a	n
s	e	g	l	a	r	a	z	a	m	u	l
l	o	n	e	g	a	n	o	g	i	l	a

The letters for these ritual implements are drawn out of this diagram by a number of different methods. For the Holy Table the letters around the perimeter of the table mostly just go down each column vertically and wrap around the table counter-clockwise with a few permutations. The letters in the center of the table are drawn from the center of the diagram.

For the lamen the letters are placed in a much more complex scheme that involves separating the diagram into three parts. It will be easier to see with Enochian letters, so here is the diagram again with its compartments.

The central rectangle is called the heart. In the holy table these letters are, with a few twists and turns, placed in the center of the hexagram, but in the lamen these same letters are placed around the edges of the inner square. The rectangle surrounding the heart is called the flesh. These letters fill the outer square of the lamen. The two vertical rectangles are called the skin. These letters are arranged to fill the central diamond of the lamen.

Unfortunately the originals of these items actuall used by Dee have been lost to posterity, perhaps destroyed, perhaps jealously guarded by some unknown collector of rarities. My version of the Holy Table is at some variance with most modern represent-ations. These are all at least in part based on the frontispiece to Meric Casaubon's *A True and Faithful…*

I have chosen not to separate the letters around the edge of the table into separate compartments. I have done this for sever-al reasons. First, Casaubon's illlustration is highly suspicious be-cause it reverses the letters at the center of the table and was constructed by an antagonist rather than enthusiast of Dee's work.

Secondly, we do have two sources for descriptions of the table that seem more reliable. We have a diagram of the table drawn by Dee in Sloane Manuscript 3189. While this diagram has some pricks around the edges of the table, it does not separate the letters into squares. These pricks seem to be placed there to measure the spaces for the letters rather than to form squares. If Dee wanted squares around each letter he would have done so. There is also a description of the table by Elias Ashmole quoted in Peterson's *John Dee's Five books of Mystery*.[1]

There are also seven symbols called "The Ensigns of Creation" that are to be placed on the table. The following diagram shows these symbols placed on the table. For a full-color representation of this image see the cover of *The Enochian Magick Toolbook*. I have chosen to color these ensigns based on the planetary color scheme of the Golden Dawn. This is not traditional, but suits my sense of magical aesthetic. These "ensigns" were some of the first visionary symbols that Dee and Kelly received, and they were never explained in any detail. Different authors have assigned them to various planets, and my own choice is to align them with the Heptarchia.

---

[1] Peterson, Joseph H. *John Dee's Five books of Mystery* p. 23

If you wish to construct your own Holy Table, the directions are that the table surface should be about 36" square. My table is actually quite a bit smaller, as space constraints make such a large altar unfeasible.

The table is supported by four legs, at the ends of which are shallow hollows in which you can fit four small versions of the Sigillum Dei Aemeth so that the table is resting on top of them. This way you are completely insulating the table from "impure' influences.

Building a table like this is far easier than it might appear. I took several shortcuts in the construction of my table and it is still quite beautiful and powerful to behold. I began by obtaining a small table. I then had a 23" X 23" poster of the above image printed.[1] I decoupaged this to a 23" square board and glued it to the top of the table. I then used gold paint to finish the image. For the legs I got four small round boxes from a craft store and glued the lids to the feet of the table. In all it took me just a few hours. It might take a bit longer if you're not a "crafty" person but it is a very beautiful altar and fills my temple with a wonderful atmosphere.

The entire apparatus is generally covered with a red silk cloth but I have not done so in the image on the back cover so that you can see the table nicely.

---

[1] I've made this available from cafepress.com or my website.

Appendix E
Enochian Magick Resources

Very early on in my magical studies I became committed to making ritual magick resources readily available to myself as well as other practicing occultists. I have created a wide number of helpful tools for Enochian Magick work that can all be found through *www.newhermetics.com* or by going directly to my online store *http://shop.vendio.com/centerofchanges/category/3034/*

These include:

The Enochian Magick Toolbook
Wax Sigillum Dei Aemeth in both large and small sizes
Various Sizes of Posters of the Four Watchtowers
Posters of the Heptarchia Mystica
Poster of The Holy Table – can be pasted onto a table for practical use
Concave Skrying Mirrors
Crystal Balls in several sizes
Candles and Incense etc.

Online Resources for further Enochian Study:

http://freepages.rootsweb.com/~cgb143/index.html
A wonderful concordance of the Enochian Language from the Keys

http://www.hermetic.com/
Various Enochian Papers and Resources including Benjamin Rowe's collected works, with numerous diaries of visions.

http://www.themagickalreview.org/
A PDF of *A True and Faithful* as well as digital scans of the
Manuscripts from the British Museum.

http://www.azothart.com
Numerous robes and other regalia for ceremonial magick.

This is not by any means a complete list of online Enochian
resources. These just happen to be a few of the ones I like. There
are many other Enochian websites, but many just contain the
same articles found in the above. There are a few other gems, but
I'll let you "google" them.

Enochian Literature Resources:

Here are some very brief reviews of some of the extent
literature on John Dee and Enochian Magick. Publishing details
of those consulted for the present text will be provided in the
bibliiography.

British Library Original Enochian Manuscripts:

Sloane 3188- Dee's magical diaries. This part covers reception of
the Ensigns of Creation, the Sigillum Dei Aemeth, the Heptarchia Mystica, the Angelic or Enochian alphabet and parts of Liber
Loagaeth. (Edited and published as *John Dee's Five Books of
Mystery.* See below).

Sloane 3189- A series of tables of numbers and letters called Liber
Loagaeth. Little information about the functional use of these
tables survives.

Sloane 3191- This seems to be Dee's personal grimoire, it contains
the 48 Angelic Keys, The Book of Earthly Science, Aid and
Victory, On the Mystic Heptarchy, and Invocations of the Good

Angels. (Largely edited and published as *The Enochian Magick of Dr. John Dee*. See below)

Cotton Appendix XLVI parts 1 and 2- Dee's Magical Diaries. This part contains the reception of 91 Governors and the Thirty Aethyrs, the Angelic or Enochian Keys, the Four Watchtowers and various adventures across the European continent. A vast number of years is missing in the middle. (Edited and published as *A True and Faithful Relation of What Passed for Many Years Between Dr. John Dee and Some Spirits*. See below).

Enochian Magick Instructional Literature:

The Equinox Volume 1, Nos. 7 and 8- Good brief accounts of the Enochian magick of the Golden Dawn. Very sketch-like coverage, and ignores Heptarchia Mystica entirely.

Enochian World of Aleister Crowley,(Enochian Sex Magick)- Mostly a reprint of the Equinox material with a useful introduction by Duquette. The supplementary material is of questionable utility, particularly the sex magick.

The Golden Dawn (Llewellyn)- Contains much of the Golden Dawn Enochian instruction, although re-ordered somewhat from the original papers. The Heptarchia Mystica is totally ignored.

The Complete Golden Dawn System of Magic (New Falcon)- This again contains the core of the Golden Dawn Enochian materials, much the same as in the Llewellyn version, and several supplementary papers by modern authors. The Heptarchia Mystica is again totally ignored.

Enochian Magic- Gerald Schueler based this work entirley on the Golden Dawn materials found in Crowley and Regardie, with numerous errors and embellishments based largely on Gematria.

The material on the Thirty Aethyrs is somewhat interesting. This work seems totally unaware of the Heptarchia Mystica.

Advanced Enochian Magic- Also by Gerald Schueler, but here the author begins to develop his own system and deviates from both the Golden Dawn and Dee's materials into something new. It's value will be up to the individual practioner to decide. Again there is still no reference to the Heptarchia Mystica.

Golden Dawn Enochian Magic- Pat Zaleski attempts to enlarge the Golden Dawn system to include more on the 30 aethyrs and governors as well as the Heptarchia. It is unclear how much of this is actual order work and how much is from the author's own work, research and magical imagination.

Enochian Magic for Beginner's- A fairly well-reseached and read-able text that attempts to offer the system as much as possible in its entirety based wholly on the original texts. However, because Dee's diaries do not contain an entire system the author is forced to fill in or leave blanks in many places.

Enochian Initiation- This book is for the most part the magical diary of a magician who conjured the Seniors of the four tablets twice in in a row successively. It is an interesting personal account, and a good example of using this work theurgically. But I would avoid taking the author's experiences or conclusions as gospel. It is highly idiosyncratic.

The Enochian Magick of Dr. John Dee (Enochian Evocation)- Largely a transcription and translation of Sloane 3191, with additions from some of Dee's journals. An excellent and readable source-book, but not without transcription errors.

John Dee's Five Books of Mystery- John Dee's early diaries (Sloane 3188), including the reception of the Sigillum Dei Aemeth and the Heptarchia Mystica.

A True and Faithful Relation of What Passed for Many Years Between Dr. John Dee and Some Spirits- An invaluable but flawed transcription of Dee's later journals including the reception of the governors and aethyrs, the forty-nine keys, and the four watchtowers. (Cotton Appendix XLVI)

Appendix F
Some Visions and Voices

I thought I should include a few of my own visions for educational purposes, largely because the angel Ave told me to do so. I have not chosen the following because they are any more or less important than other visions, my own or those of others. I have chosen these largely because they are relatively brief, while containing some useful information that may help you with your own process. And they were all received using the exact techniques outlined in this book.

It may be interesting to note that many things communicated to me in these visions are not part of my personal beliefs or ways that I often think at all. There is a mildly Christian undertone in one or two of them, and I have never been a Christian. This theme has come up in several other visions as well. Some of the beings I encounter seem warm toward me, and others do not. One of the angels in the following visions seems to think I am something of a failure and a hypocrite. Another seems to want me to be some sort of messiah. Neither of these are roles I aspire toward particularly. The angels seem to have an agenda of their own quite frequently, and my original intentions become diluted or sometimes even ignored. Some elements of the communications, both those recorded here and many others, are still somewhat mysterious to me.

Some of these visions resulted from looking into a concave black mirror, and others were conducted with my eyes closed. All of these visions were recorded on audiotape and I have not edited them except for clarity in a few places. Because of this, these records also show one of the inherent difficulties of working alone, which is that when in an altered state sometimes quite obvious questions seem to be forgotten or missed and one's consciousness is more childlike. The visions also generally commence with some somewhat random images, sometimes related, other times not so much. In places I slip into such a deep trance that what exactly transpired is lost in mumbling or silence. But here is a small sampling of some of my practical work.

Vision of the Son of the Son of Light *Ave*

I see the reddish light behind my eyes, shapes form, speckles of glitter, I see a star and a silver chalice, I see a tree, a slender tree with wide branches, I grow closer and it's transforming into a ball of light.

"Ave! Zacar od Zamran Ave!" I see a bunch of different shapes, writing is being erased, I get the feeling that something is communicating that I've erased the sigillum dei aemeth and I need to remake it before I can contact anything well. "But I insist Ave..."

I see a shape, almost looks like... something's changed... ---a silent interlude of deep trance for approximately two minutes--- I see a pentagram, I feel myself shifting, my "wavelength changing." I see the number 4 and some coils, I see some random shapes- now some angel wings, soft and white, birdlike, a white robed figure, golden hair, curling, very serene face, very young looking,

"Ave?"

"It is I," he says.

"Ave... (some incomprehensible utterances)" "Ave can you take me to your realm so that we can communicate better?"

He takes hold of me, we are rising up... we arrive at a stoney hill. He sets us down- he's got a light shining from him fairly brightly- it's difficult to entirely make him out. I ask him if I can feel his essence. I touch his chest. I feel his warmth, the softness of his robe, and I feel us join- our connection- joyful, I ask him if there is anything in my book that needs improvement in terms of accuracy and effectiveness.

Include more examples from my own work that would portray what my experiences are, and that I shouldn't rush to press, "There is much to learn, and much will be learned."

"Can you show me anything new?" I ask.

He shows me a sphere with a triangle in it, or rather a triangle with a sphere on it, a sphere sitting on a triangle, it's got seven levels, and each of the levels has some letters on it, They seem to be the letters of the Sigillum Dei Aemeth. (those around the outer heptagon)

"What is this?" I ask.

He says, "It's another way of approaching the visions," That if you were to place a crystal ball atop this, it could be used outside of the circle for contacting other beings and evil spirits. I ask him why I would call evil spirits, and he says, "You should never call evil spirits." He shakes his finger. "It is for calling vast hierarchies many of which have never been revealed,"

"Will these be revealed to me?" I ask.

He says he is not sure, if I prove myself worthy, perhaps. I see a "T," A large capital "T,"

"What is this?" I ask.

"That is the pommel of a sword of righteousness with which the wicked are smited."

"Where is the sword?" I ask.

He says, "the sword is in the hand of him who will vanquish the forces of darkness. Visions can be mere mental games, but there is a real war."

Behind him I see many other angelic figures looking at me. "Who are these?"

"They are my brothers and sisters. You must invoke each one of them and learn the secrets that have never been revealed. If you would have knowledge."

"But what of my book?" I ask.

"It is well, but this is not your true work. Your true work is to help rectify all that which is fallen into disorder and decay."

315

"But I am just an artist," I say.

"You are a leader of men. You are a leader of men! You will be given an army and with this army you can rebuild the beautiful image of the heavens on earth." I see a symbol- a hexagram with a circle in the middle. "It is well," he says.

"Is there more today?"

No.

"Thank you Ave and all the angels of Light, I will communicate with each of you."

"Your army is on earth and in the heavens."

"Thank you." – What a strange vision!

Vision of the Thirtieth Aethyr *Tex*

I see some swirling colors in front of me- I rise up into them, I'm beginning to see some figures, I feel somewhat loose- I see some shapes swirling around in the darkness-

I go through a gateway with the letters TEX, on the other side of the gateway I see something of a landscape in front of me, some sharp-peaked hills. I reach down and touch the sand. It's reddish, grainy, the landscape is somewhat alien, strange rock formations, they form gates and bridges, joining each other forming sort of hoops in the sand. I touch the rock's surface. It's warm and hard, not smooth and yet not overly rough. I move through this sort of labyrinth of peaks looking for something of interest here.

As I move further along I see what appears to be a walled village of some sort, or no a citadel, almost appears to be a cathedral, I move closer to this place, it seems to be sort of bluish-purplish in color, spires pointing up into the sky. I grow closer, a few steps lead inside, through a somewhat rounded opening. The rocks are smooth almost semi-translucent.

I step within, find myself in a hall with square stones forming the floor, pillars on either side. There seem to be some sort of animals wandering in the hall. There is a raised platform with stairs. I move forward, across the smooth stone floor. It's quite cool in here.

And on the dais I see a man in warrior clothes, a helmet with wings, forming a visor. I can't see his face too well, it seems to be a hard and strange-looking face. I draw closer, he's wearing armor. He has the wings of an angel. I greet him and shine light at him.

"I am your brother," I say to him.

"I am the Vast Countenance. A hundred thousand legions of angels serve beneath me," he says.

I ask him where they are.

"They are here." I look around, and I discover the very pillars and walls of this place are made up of a myriad of beings. And he says "If you wish to know the mystery of the Aethyr, it is that beingness and becomingness are linked by the causal factors of existence. All things are alive in this place, everything is of intelligence and beingness." He grows and he seems to have some alien components to parts of his body, then like he's a great serpent made of fire.

The whole cathedral and everything has come to pieces and a vast number of beings in concentric circles surround him. He's become so big that I can't really speak to him any further. I approach one of the beings, a very elf-like angel, glowing. I ask her name.

"Ladia, angel of the one countenance." She says she is part of that which holds the appearance of all things together. Her essence is of the one. Her true appearance is like beams of light.

Everything is now dissolving into light. As the image resolves itself I see an island floating in a sea. It's sort of like a mountain, hard, with a flat peak at the top. Vegetation below, but a large rock. I go down to the rock. As I get there, there is a pegasus flying horse on the rock. I ask its name "Maretri-(something)." (I become distracted by thoughts about various names)

I find myself riding the horse, and it's taking me across a crystalline landscape, like a vast field of jutting quartz crystals, we're riding along the ground and then his wings spread and we take off a little bit into the air and I see crystals as far as the eye can see. And a huge one is ahead of us. We come to the base of it. There is a gateway into the crystal itself.

The horse leaves me at this gateway. I move within. The light through the crystal makes the passageway seem to glow. I see some beings. It's rather difficult to identify what they are. They seem to be robed, walking through the passageway and they take really no notice of me. I keep moving through passageway.

I come to a man with a white robe and a long white beard. He seems to be glowing. He's got a kind face. I greet him. He greets me.

"What is your name?" I ask.

"I am the spirit of eventide. In the space between the worlds, I greet those in the darkness with a ray of light. You are lost, and I will help you to find your way." He points behind him and there is a screen or gateway leading into a field of green, a prairie or valley, very green and nice and there's a path of stones (round, granite).

I thank him for pointing in this new direction and I go upon the path and I walk into this land of green. And there is a very giant being. I can only see his legs at first- he appears to be made of crystal or liquid glass. I look up and I see that he's armed. He asks me what I'm doing here. I hesitantly say that the spirit of eventide sent me. He says that I've come far, and have entered the land of plenteous earth and that I'm welcome to wander its hills and valleys, but that I must not take or touch anything. He waves me past him. I ask him his name- Mordrax (?)

I follow the stone path for quite some time but it doesn't seem to lead anywhere. I rise up into the air and see in the great distance what appears to be a city. But as I grow closer it becomes clear that what I see is actually a series of cylindrical shapes of various sizes, and that within these shapes are beings.

I look around to find someone to explain this to me and I see a large jungle cat, perhaps a cheetah. I ask if he could explain this place to me. He shakes his head and points off to his right where I see a greenish glow amongst the cylinders.

I approach the glow and there is an elf-like female. Margana (?)

I ask her what this place was she says "These are the souls of those who are lost due to emphasizing discipline above joy. Mark this well, that your endeavors should join discipline and pleasure." I then felt compelled to end the vision.

Vision of the Daughter of Light *Akele*

I see a face, small, slight chin, thin nose, almost Christina-Ricci-like, but more classicly beautiful, wavy hair,

"Akele?" the field of view becomes hazy, many points of light, the mirror obscured, I see something forming, the shape of a woman almost floating, her arms spread. "Akele? Is that you?"

Her voice is high, "It is I."

"You're very far away. Wouldn't you like to come closer?" Instantly she is quite close, half in the mirror, half beyond the mirror. It's the same face as before. She's wearing a grayish shining robe. She's almost projected in front of the mirror now, the image is small.

"What do you want of me?" she says.

"I want to understand more," I say.

"You have much understanding, but you understand nothing. There is little to understand," she says. I see a pathway in front of me, between twin arches, pointed, almost glass arches- a geometric triangular shape. She is standing in the midst. "This is the point of balance." I can't understand some things she's saying, and then she says something about my state needing to be more altered for us to communicate effectively.

"Do you wish to communicate with me?" I ask.

"I wish to communicate with all who would listen. These are secrets, but they are open secrets. Anyone who would come to me is worthy of these secrets."

"What secrets are you referring to?" I ask.

"The secrets of creation. The secrets of the manifest universe."

My image of her is fading in and out, and her shape is changing. "Can you help to draw me deeper into the vision?" I ask.

"That is not my way," she says.

"Do any of the Daughters or Sons of Light help with that?"

"Beigia… Stimcul…"

"The Son or the Daughter?" I ask.

"The Daughter of course," she says, laughing.

"I wish to be more transported into your world."

"That is not for today." I see what looks like an hourglass or perhaps a dorje, she says it's a thunderbolt. "This is my power," she says.

"The sixth heaven?"

"No," she says, "That's not right. I am amongst the creatures of the Earth. I rule under the heavens in the name of him who created all things."

I'm seeing a sphere with wings, silver.

She comes very close to the mirror's edge, and says severely, "What do you want?" scowling.

"I am sincerely seeking wisdom and knowledge," I say.

"Why do you play at trifles then?"

"I don't know. I am not trying to do anything but communicate."

"Where is your concentration?" she asks.

"I'm just trying to be open," I reply.

"Your mind must be like a single ray of light, but relaxed, sharp as a knife, as calm as a babe asleep." I'm seeing her as a winged being now, with a diamond-shape at her chest, and her hands are held in the shape a square in front of her, framing the diamond. She's now quite tall, and the diamond is blue, and behind her are many others, and there is a mountain. At the top of the mountain is a watchtower. "I am she of the river in the night. I am the lady of the swan and of the turtledove. The moon is no stranger to me." I see a cross. "Born under God, there is no number but one. There is no God but one. And in him are three persons. Here is wisdom. Here is wonder. Here is hope. You are the elect of the elect. You have been chosen from amongst the many for the knowledge of the eternal. No name can encompass the entirety. There is no religion that does not make mock of god, twisting god into a puppet for the priests on the path to worldly power. Let no man mistake this for god. Here is wisdom. Wise as serpents must you be, in the path to eternity. All is folly save the One. These words are skew-wise, heed them carefully, there is a riddle herein."

I am seeing some incomprehensible images, bubbles containing scenes- or angels. It is too much to take in. What I'm seeing is not a normal experience. She seems to have left.

"Thank you Akele."

Vision of **Sias** from Water of Air

I see a good deal of movement in the mirror, a lot of swirling shapes, like flowing fabric, angelic shapes mingling and disappearing but nothing to hold on to yet...

I see a plain, a field with scrubby grass. Very dried and parched, and in the distance I see a gray lake and behind that a mountain.

"Zacar od zamran ils gah Sias!" I look around the field and by the lake I see a figure holding what looks like a vase, very similar to "Temperance" but without wings. The face is very much like a Greek statue. As I go closer I see the being's hair is glowing, almost on fire. His eyes are quite fierce.

"What would you have of me?" he says.

"I've come for knowledge," I reply. "You've come to the right place. There's little I cannot help you with," he says. "Though I do not feel moved to help you much," he adds. He appears to be cleaning the vase.

"What is that vase for?" I ask.

"It is a vessel of universal medicine, and no I will not be sharing that with you today."

"I seek understanding regarding some areas of my life."

"You're life is a disaster. You have been inconsistent in all things to do with your life. You have not practiced what you've preached, and yet you lord over others. Humble yourself before the Lord, and then this knowledge will go aright." He showed me a tablet filled with letters and numbers, four by four with a cross running through it diagonally.

He tells me that this is the answer to what I seek.

"What do I seek that has to do with this?" I ask.

"The manner of balancing yourself."

"Is this a talisman? How is it to be made?" I ask.

He says that the traditional methods will suffice.

"Yellow flashing with purple, would that be appropriate?" I ask.

"That would be perfection."

"What is this place that I am looking at?" I ask, referring to the field.

"It is the plain (plane?) of sorrow." He seems taciturn and more interested in his vase than communicating any more with me.

"Thank you Sias."

Vision of *Babalel (Minister Onedpon)*

The mirror is filled with red light and triangular forms, coming in and out of focus, interlocking triangles, (?) thick sharp, I see a cross, turned over on its side, diagonally facing, I see what almost looks like an "Indian Chief" – I'm seeing a vesica of light, sparks of light coming out of the mirror, nothing forming coherently yet.

I see a stone pyramid, cracked, its smooth and shiny, I seem to be passing through it. I'm in an underground place, a momentary flash of a fisherman, I see some boiling magma.

I hear a voice- "Here is the answer to your question."

"Where are you king Babalel?" I ask.

"I haven't the time to speak with you, call one of my ministers," says the still disembodied voice.

"Zacare od Zamran ils gah Onedpon dooiap Babalel od Befafes zacar od zamran Onedpon." A face is immediately in the mirror. A changeable face. "Are you Onedpon?"

The face disappears.

I then see an older man with bushy hair, he's wearing long boots, and a military looking cloak and tunic.

"Onedpon?"

"The Same."

"I'm trying to understand today why Babalel and Befafes are rulers of the sea."

"You have received your answer. They are the rulers of all combustible substances and violence."

The vision fades a bit. I'm seeing a number of different things. Swirling energies. I'm going through a tunnel. Onedpon seems to have gone. I find myself on a barren landscape.

Onedpon is there and says, "You wished for more of an answer to your question."

I see an eagle, or, a pelican?

"Is this answer alchemical?" I ask.

I see the sign of sulfur ($\overset{\triangle}{+}$) I see some red clouds in a round glass vessel, and there's a red dragon in the vessel among the clouds and it's going to sleep, as it goes to sleep it turns into a black liquid, and then I see the seal of Liba, and out of the vessel comes a mighty red and black angel.

And I hear a voice say, "Too soon, too soon." It all disappears.

I'm in a black field with a red pentagram on the ground. Everything else is gone. And I'm beginning to see a being that looks like a wizard, but he seems strange to me so I will end.

Bibliography

Agrippa, Henry Cornelius. *Three Books of Occult Philosophy* (St. Paul, MN; Llewellyn Books, 1993)

Casaubon, Meric. *A True and Faithful Relation of What Passed for Many Years Between Dr. John Dee and Some Spirits* (London, England: D. Maxwell for T. Garthwait, 1659)

Crowley, Aleister. *The Equinox Vols. 1-10* (York Beach, ME: Samuel Weiser Books, 1999)

———. *Magick: Book 4 Liber ABA* (York Beach, ME: Samuel Weiser Books, 1998)

———. *The Vision and the Voice* (York Beach, ME: Samuel Weiser Books, 1998)

Duquette, Lon Milo. *Enochian World of Aleister Crowley (Enochian Sex Magick)* (Phoenix, AZ: New Falcon Publications, 1991)

French, Peter J. *John Dee: The World of an Elizabethan Magus* (London, UK: Camelot Press, 1972)

Harkness, Deborah E. *John Dee's Conversations with Angels* (Cambridge, UK: Cambridge University Press, 1999)

James, Geoffrey. *The Enochian Magick of Dr. John Dee* (St. Paul, MN: Llewellyn Books, 1994) (Originally published as *Enochian Evocation*)

Newcomb, Jason Augustus. *21st Century Mage* (Boston, MA: Weiser Books, 2002)

———. *The New Hermetics* (Boston, MA: Weiser Books, 2004)

———. *Sexual Sorcery* (Boston, MA: Weiser Books, 2005)

———. *The Book of Magick Power* (Sarasota, FL: New Hermetics Press, 2007)

Peterson, Joseph H. *John Dee's Five Books of Mystery* (Boston, MA: Weiser Books, 2003)

Ptolemy, Claudius. *Tetrabiblos, Loeb Classical Library, Volume 1* (Cambridge, MA: Harvard University Press, 1940)

Regardie, Israel. *The Complete Golden Dawn System of Magic* (Phoenix, AZ: New Falcon Publications, 1990)

————. *The Golden Dawn* (St. Paul, MN: Llewellyn Books, 1986)

Schueler, Gerald and Betty. *Enochian Magic* (St. Paul, MN: Llewellyn Books, 1985)

Schueler, Gerald J. *An Advanced Guide to Enochian Magic* (St. Paul, MN: Llewellyn Books, 1987)

Smith, Charlotte Fell. *John Dee* (York Beach, ME: Ibis Press, 2004)

Tyson, Donald. *Enochian Magick for Beginners* (St. Paul, MN: Llewellyn Books, 1992)

Wenger, Win. *The Einstein Factor* (Roseville, CA: Prima Publishing, 1996)

Woolley, Benjamin. *The Queen's Conjurer* (New York, NY: Henry Holt, 2001)

Zalewski, Pat. *Golden Dawn Enochian Magic* (St. Paul, MN: Llewellyn Books, 1990)

About the Author

Jason Augustus Newcomb has been studying and practicing Enochian Magick since 1986. He has devoted his life to gaining and sharing an increased understanding of the Western Mystery Tradition, both how it relates to modern consciousness studies, and its relations with other forms of esoteric spirituality. Jason is a long-time initiate of Western Mystery Schools, both visible and invisible, and has explored magic and mysticism in its varied forms for the past twenty-two or so years... in this incarnation. Jason's goal is to participate in the evolution of humanity in whatever small way Divine Providence has ordained for him. He is devoted to helping people expand both personally and spiritually, seeing these as essentially in the same continuum. He is the author of the books: *21st Century Mage, The New Hermetics, Sexual Sorcery,* and *The Book of Magick Power;* and has produced an extensive series of audio CDs offering instruction in magical practice and hypnosis. He is also a licensed Neuro-Linguistic Programming Practitioner a certified Clinical Hypnotherapist. In his most creative moments he is also a painter, sculptor, novelist, screen-writer and filmmaker. Jason now lives with his wife Jennifer and their daughter Aurora in Sarasota, FL.

You can visit Jason's website at www.newhermetics.com for more information.

Printed in the United States
103886LV00002B/84/A

9 780615 177090